FROM SWASTIKA TO JIM CROW
Refugee Scholars at Black Colleges

FROM SWASTIKA TO JIM CROW
Refugee Scholars at Black Colleges

Gabrielle Simon Edgcomb

KRIEGER PUBLISHING COMPANY
MALABAR, FLORIDA

Original Edition 1993

Printed and Published by
KRIEGER PUBLISHING COMPANY
KRIEGER DRIVE
MALABAR, FLORIDA 32950

Library of Congress Cataloging-In-Publication Data

Edgcomb, Gabrielle Simon.
  From Swastika to Jim Crow: Refugee Scholars at Black Colleges /
  Gabrielle Simon Edgcomb. — Original ed.
      p.   cm.
  Includes bibliographical references and index.
  ISBN 0–89464–775–X (acid-free paper)
  1. Afro-American universities and colleges—Faculty—History—20th
century.   2. Refugees, Political—United States—History—20th
century.   3. Refugees, Jewish—United States—History—20th century.
I. Title.
LC2781.E34   1993
378.73'08996'073—dc20   92-20752
                                                                  CIP

10 9 8 7 6 5

CONTENTS

DEDICATION

In loving memory of my mother, Hedwig Simon, whose courage and wisdom gave me life twice by bringing us out of Nazi Germany in time.

FOREWORD

One of the remarkable stories of refugees during World War II is that of scholars, largely Jewish, who found opportunities to pursue their professions in historically black colleges in the United States. They represented a variety of academic disciplines and brought to their new homeland experiences from central and eastern Europe that were, in some ways, similar to those that they would have in the land of Jim Crow.

There have been no accounts from the refugees themselves, even though those who had the experiences were not only numerous but were, for the most part, also unusually articulate. They could well have recounted their own experiences had they chosen to do so. One wonders why they did not. An obvious reason is that the difficulties of coping with their new environment was all-consuming and, consequently, left little or no time for telling others what they were encountering. Another reason is, of course, the personal pain they would go through in narrating yet another example of bigotry in whatever form it took in their adopted home. Had they come so far in their effort to escape humiliation and degradation only to find it very much alive in the land of the free and the home of the brave? Or, perhaps, it was because they did not wish to draw attention to themselves, thus inviting the opprobrium of the dominant group that would be too reminiscent of the land from which they had fled. It is unfortunate that, for whatever reason, none of these refugees, many of them so gifted, has provided a first-hand account of the years they spent teaching in historically black colleges and universities.

Happily, this deficiency has been remedied not by one of the refugees but by one unusually well qualified by birth, training, and experience

to do so. Gabrielle Simon Edgcomb, the author of this work, was born
and educated (until age fifteen) in Germany. Although she had escaped
the harshness and savage treatment from which many Jews suffered, she
had learned of the anti-Semitism that was becoming more rampant in
the 1930s, when she emigrated to the United States. She was most
fortunate in being able to emigrate to the United States before experi-
encing the extreme manifestations of anti-Semitism. While quite young
when she came to this country, she was fully prepared to understand
and appreciate not only the suffering of Jews in Germany but also the
harrowing experiences they would have in relocating in the United
States.

By the time she had adjusted to her new life in the United States and
had become acquainted with some of the refugees who taught at black
colleges and universities, as well as with African Americans themselves,
she was in a position to undertake the task of writing about their
experiences at such institutions.

Some African Americans like myself, who have long had connections
with historically black colleges and universities, have been very interested in the impact of the refugees on the intellectual life of these
institutions. Some of us have known these refugees as teachers, colleagues, professional associates, and friends. We have appreciated the
role they have played in breaking down racial barriers in the communities where the black educational institutions were located, in maintaining rigorous standards in their own scholarship and in the scholarship
of their students, and in the general respect they accorded their African
American students and colleagues.

It is well to remember that these historically black institutions did
not impose any color barriers whatsoever. They were always open to
students of whatever race, whenever the law permitted; and there were
numerous occasions when the law allowed the mixing of races at such
places when it would be countenanced nowhere else. These institutions
almost always had whites on the faculty, and they were not always
from the North. Indeed, the historically black colleges and universities
were about the only places in Jim Crow America where white Americans and African Americans could communicate on the basis of equality
and mutual respect.

Even so, the majority of these refugee educators found themselves in
a virtually impossible situation. As white professors in black institutions, they were regarded as an integral part of the life of the black

college community. As white people in a community that was racially segregated, they were looked on with suspicion by blacks if they mingled freely with whites, and they were regarded as peculiar by whites if their social life was spent among blacks. It was asking a great deal of anyone to cope with this incredibly complex social situation. It was asking too much of refugees from Nazi Germany to display total equanimity in the process. While not all of them were overwhelmingly successful, many threw themselves into their work, became important contributors to the intellectual and social life of their institutions, and had a permanent, positive impact on innumerable students.

Edgcomb has performed an important task in recapturing the story of this remarkable group of men and women, and in reminding us that in the human family there are those who can transcend the Nazi Swastika as well as Jim Crow, and set an example of civilized human relations that their students and colleagues would do well to emulate.

John Hope Franklin
James B. Duke Professor of
  History Emeritus
Duke University
Durham, North Carolina

PREFACE

"Unsung Heroes"

This work concerns the stories of the exiled scholars from Germany and Austria who came to the United States as victims of Nazi policies and came to hold faculty positions in historically black colleges. These scholars had achieved their professional status at German or Austrian universities and were members of the faculty or staff at professional institutions. They had been dismissed from their posts as victims of Nazi racist policies or, in some instances, for their opposition to the regime. They had come to understand that they must reassemble the pieces of their lives and careers in exile in a foreign land with an alien culture, using a new language.

I have identified fifty-one individuals and nineteen institutions which figure in this story. The copious and growing body of pertinent exile literature contains no mention of an investigation of this significant episode in minority and immigration history:

> Those who chose or were forced to choose to teach in small southern colleges, both black and white, were often the first ambassadors of European culture in these settings. They remain the unsung heroes of American higher education. I nevertheless decided not to concern myself with such persons, even though I feel that there is an urgent need to assess their impact.[1]

Professor Ernst Manasse, who taught German, Latin and philosophy at North Carolina Central College (now University) in Durham, North

Carolina, from 1939 to 1973, and whose wife, Marianne Manasse, taught German there as well, elaborated:

> ... whereas a number of people are inclined to say friendly things about the contributions we refugee scholars made to the growth and development of several predominantly Black Colleges, both my wife and I felt that the experiences we made at these institutions changed and enriched our lives in significant ways, both intellectually and emotionally.[2]

The significance of this historical episode lies in the encounter between two diverse groups of people, both victims of extreme manifestations of racist oppression and persecution, albeit under vastly different historical conditions. The Europeans came out of a middle-class, intellectual environment of high status and expectations prior to the disaster. African Americans at that time were two and three generations removed from slavery, under which even learning to read had been generally forbidden.

My investigation has brought to light revealing experiences of both participants in this encounter, inevitably of considerable impact on both the individuals and institutions concerned. Illustrative stories, anecdotes and observations of these developments are presented in the hope that the work will contribute to cross-cultural understanding in American society as the twentieth century closes.

In 1980, the Smithsonian Institution's Office of Symposia and Seminars held a colloquium called "The Muses Flee Hitler" on the occasion of the centenary of Albert Einstein's birth. It concerned the luminaries of this group of exile scholars, such as Einstein, Thomas and Heinrich Mann and Bertolt Brecht.

I approached Ms. Carla Borden, the editor of the subsequently published eponymous book, then associate director of the Office, with my idea of pursuing the possibility of identifying enough refugee scholars in black colleges to justify a study. She agreed to seek support from the Smithsonian to explore the matter and succeeded to the extent of enabling us to begin. The Office's director, Dr. Wilton Dillon, enthusiastically supported the project and we had the logistical resources we needed to start. We sent letters of inquiry to nearly a hundred historically black colleges and placed advertisements in the *New York Times Book Review* and the *Aufbau*, a German-language newspaper founded in 1934 by and for German Jewish refugees.

Based upon the replies received, we decided to proceed and discovered increasing numbers of names and other useful data. We visited several libraries and a few campuses and continued to collect documentary material and to conduct interviews and correspondence.

It soon became clear that the results of our exploration indeed justified a systematic effort of research and documentation, as well as interviews with the principals, former students and other witnesses. Despite the unfortunate fact that this work would have borne more fruit twenty years ago, enough significant evidence has been collected to make this project worthwhile.

Our joint work could not continue for long, as Ms. Borden's time for this side-occupation became increasingly limited and the funds allocated, merely sufficient for the early exploration, were soon spent. I proceeded by myself, continuing the research with the ongoing logistical support of the Smithsonian and some assistance from the Phelps-Stokes Fund, which had designated me a Resident Scholar in order to enable me to complete this work. Regrettably, negligible funding materialized. Faced with insufficient resources to do the research and complete the project, I had ruefully decided to abandon the work. Then, chance led me to the newly established German Historical Institute. Dr. Hartmut Lehmann, the Institute's director, found the subject of sufficient interest to secure the necessary support to enable me to complete the project.

The Institute's focus, among other subjects, also addresses German immigrant history from all periods, and two additional projects on the Nazi period refugees have been pursued. At first, I was able to continue the research as a staff member of the Institute for eight months in 1988; nine months later, a stipend for twenty-one months was secured from the Deutsche Forschungsgemeinschaft for the purpose of completing the research and preparing this manuscript. I would also like to thank Peter Kovler for his generous support.

Aside from the aforementioned Ms. Carla Borden, Dr. Wilton Dillon and Professor Hartmut Lehmann, I want to acknowledge the unfailing courtesy, support, and substantive help I received from my colleagues at the German Historical Institute, especially in rescuing me from my computer illiteracy on many occasions.

Special thanks must go to Ms. Suzanne Groff. She transcribed all the audiotapes, some of them very difficult to understand. She also provided computer services and other invaluable assistance toward the preparation of the manuscript under sometimes trying circumstances.

NOTES

1. Lewis A. Coser, *Refugee Scholars in America: Their Impact and Their Experiences* (New Haven: Yale University Press, 1984), p. xiv.
2. Letter from Ernst Manasse to Carla Borden, June 14, 1984.

INTRODUCTION

"Don't Ride with the Tribe!"

I have frequently been asked how I came to pursue this subject. The very remarkable and effective civil rights activist, Julius Hobson, functioned in Washington in a variety of activities and was elected to the city council not long before he met his tragic early death in 1977. On the occasion of a celebration of this brilliant leader not long before his passing, he spoke eloquently of the scholars he had known in his graduate studies at Howard University and singled out several who had changed his world view, giving special praise to Otto Nathan and Kurt Braun, German refugee economists. Hearing this and speaking with Julius Hobson subsequently led me to wonder if there were other refugee scholars in addition to those at Howard.

I was myself a Jewish refugee youngster from Berlin who arrived in New York in 1936. Because of these German connections, I was aware of several refugee professors at Howard, since I had lived in Washington, D.C., since the 1950s.

This work is inextricably connected to my life experience, both in Berlin and in this country. In my early childhood, the Berlin Zoo offered a favorite excursion site with my father. One Sunday we saw a prominently displayed poster, "See the Real African Lip Negroes in the Zoo." There was an enclosure behind a low fence where there were groups of people, apparently families with children, with posters advertising the show and assuring the curious that they were "living in real African huts," supposedly representing a "real African village," exhibited on a European tour.

They were Ubangi people, whose lower lips were extended two or three inches by wooden disks, which made them appear to smile. I remember being horrified, not by the people themselves, but by their being on exhibit in the familiar zoo, behind a fence, where I normally came to observe animals. It is my first recollection of seeing black people. I knew that there were people of different colors in this world, but I did not attach any meaning to this knowledge.

I grew up in a secular family with little consciousness of being a Jew, until I heard the word anti-Semite and asked my parents the meaning of the new word. Their replies caused me to read some Jewish history and literature, but Jewishness was not a central concern until the Nazi takeover instantly and radically changed our lives. For me, its immediate consequence in school was segregation, the loss of friends and the departure of relatives and friends who feared for their safety.

Segregation transformed our social and cultural lives. We no longer attended the public institutions, but patronized the *Kulturbund Deutscher Juden* for performances of plays, concerts, operas and other presentations. This institution was newly formed under official sponsorship to emphasize and promote social segregation. It was still possible in Berlin to go to public performances, but it was against my family's principles to patronize institutions whose Jewish performers had been dismissed. Thus, racial segregation was a very real, personal developmental experience for me.

A memory which remains etched into my mind may be worth mentioning here. I was beginning to look a little bit like a woman and was walking on a Berlin street, when an SS man approached me and asked me if he could accompany me home. It was winter time, and I had to open my coat in order to hold up a small gold Star of David I had begun to wear on a little gold chain around my neck. Little did I fathom that a few years hence I would have to wear a yellow star under different circumstances. "You are picking the wrong race," I said, furious. The SS man roared with laughter and said, "you might as well get used to it," and walked on. I puzzled over what I should get used to exactly, but if he meant being an outcast, I was utterly determined that this was an outrageous, impossible suggestion. Get used to that? Never.

Shortly after our arrival in New York in 1936, I was enrolled at Julia Richman High School, a huge (by my standards) public girls' school. I was enthralled at being in America and enthusiastic about everything

American, not surprising under the circumstances, since I was fifteen and had suffered through three years of Nazi tyranny and terror.

I was unprepared for the size and character of Julia Richman and its racial, ethnic and class heterogeneity. Having no comprehension of American demography, I immediately decided to get to know and befriend the black girls. I perceived this as a vital step in my speedy Americanization—an obligation, as well as another new phenomenon to satisfy my voracious need to understand and become part of this amazing new world. America was discovery and wonder.

The black girls sat together in the classroom, in the cafeteria and got into "their own" subway car. I tried to join them and I talked to them in my passable English. I was met not by noticeable hostility, but by opaque, smiling silences. I could make no connection. I was disturbed and baffled until a white girl spoke to me to tell me not to "ride with the tribe" one afternoon on the subway platform—my first but not my last rebuke upon challenging racist practices. I was distressed.

I identified with these segregated second-class citizens out of my experience and upbringing. It took a long time to learn of the enormous gulf separating a middle-class European from African Americans of the period and the limitations for an individual to swim against the stream, especially for a newcomer to the peculiar American contradiction between egalitarian rhetoric and unequal reality. It took time to gain insight into this basic and tragic American conflict and the nearly insurmountable barriers which had to be transcended.

Like most new immigrants then, I knew little about the United States beyond impressions gained from reading Mark Twain, Fenimore Cooper, Sinclair Lewis and a few other authors, seeing some films and absorbing bits of information, none designed to help me relate to the African American experience. I knew there had been slavery in the South, that equality had not been realized in Mississippi and Alabama, but I was shocked and baffled by what I experienced in New York.

The struggle against the legacy of slavery and continuing endemic racism has accompanied me all my life and I have tried to be actively engaged in that struggle in a variety of ways. This commitment mandates a study of American history as it is intertwined with the African American experience and culture—not two separate "histories"—and a conscious, active pursuit of ways leading to the equality so long promised.

CHAPTER 1

"Too Many and Too Different"

After many centuries of a Jewish presence in what became the second German Reich in 1871, the federal legal system for the whole country was adopted as the basis for the emancipation of the Jews on April 16, 1871.[1] Jews constituted roughly 1 percent of the population of some 50 million. In 1933, the proportion remained the same: 60 million Germans, 600,000 Jews. German Jews were predominantly urban dwellers, as opposed to the majority of the Christian population, then mainly rural.[2]

By Nazi reckoning, all but two of the exiles in this study were "non-Aryan," i.e., they had at least one Jewish grandparent. The two "Aryans" were Erika Thimey, who had come to the United States before 1933, had returned in 1936, and, as a dancer ready to enter Berlin stage life, found the situation intolerable and emigrated for good. The other "Aryan" was Julius Lips, who found Nazi policies incompatible with his work as director of the Rautenstrauch-Joest Anthropological Museum in Cologne and fled to Paris in 1934.

I find little mention of this issue of Jewishness in the interviews and documents at hand and am going by names and the fates these people suffered.

The presence of Jewish faculty in German universities was a relatively new phenomenon, dating from the second half of the nineteenth century and increasing until 1933. The percentage of Jewish academicians was 7.1 percent of the population in 1895. In 1933, it was 12.5 percent.[3] Their situation in terms of anti-Semitism varied according to discipline and university, as well as the disposition of individuals in influential positions. There were ugly episodes before 1933 staged by members of the Nazi student organizations, always loud and threatening, sometimes violent. There had also been anti-Semitic manifestations by other students, sometimes connected with the old fraternities, which, as in the United States, were segregated into Jewish and Christian organizations.

There were no established student quotas for Jews. Exclusion and discrimination were therefore a function of specific circumstances. There can be no statement concerning the scholars in this study, as there has been no information available of their experiences of anti-Semitism in pre-Nazi Germany.

Paradoxically, in America there was "formal" discrimination, at least until World War II, which is to say that there were student quotas for Jews in some universities and professional schools and exclusion in others. Quotas were virtually universal in medical schools and Jews were rarely found in engineering. It was "common knowledge" that there were no jobs for Jewish engineers, or at least that was the assumption, although there were undoubtedly exceptions. There were, consequently, a number of Jews who pursued Ph.Ds. in various biological sciences in the hope of improving their chances of getting into medical school subsequently. Thus, the widespread belief that Jews were very studious was confirmed, sometimes meant as a compliment, sometimes not.

Few Jews enrolled in American universities in significant numbers until the 1920s and 1930s. Before then it was the descendants of the German Jews who had come to the United States in mid-nineteenth century and were more compatible with their American fellow citizens of the same class than the East Europeans who arrived later. Some earlier immigrants had achieved considerable economic and class status and were thus acceptable to the WASP males who dominated the academic power structures. The children of East European ghetto Jews were still striving to attain the requisite standards of living to aspire to a university education.

This influx of East European Jews was greeted with dismay not only by the "Blue Bloods" but with anxiety by the German Jewish "aristocracy," fearful of the specter of anti-Semitism, ever present, becoming more virulent as a reaction to these unassimilated newcomers from a world very different from the Europe they knew. It must be remembered that German Jews from mid-nineteenth century until 1933 lived inside German society to a large extent. The wealthy "Uptown Jews" of New York were "ashamed of the appearance, the language (Yiddish), and the manners of the Russian Jews, aghast at their political ideologies and terrified lest the world crumble by the mad act of a Jewish radical."

"Too many—1.5 million between 1900 and 1914—and too different," the new immigrants were playing havoc with the assimilationist vision and timetable.[4]

The newcomers had lived in ghettos or "shtetels," Jewish villages, almost entirely segregated from the general population, speaking their own language, practicing a different, despised religion and even worked in occupations reserved for them because of exclusion from others, in a hostile, dangerous environment with frequent violence and bloodshed on the part of their neighbors, as well as agents of the state. It is useful to keep in mind that Jews were considered a separate nationality in Russia then, as they still are today.

A number of German Jews had achieved faculty status at the "Big Three"—Harvard, Yale and Princeton. A few had become significant financial contributors to Harvard and had endowed chairs in their names, thus gaining influence in the university governing structures. Harvard was the first to have its restrictive policies publicized in the early twenties during President A. Lawrence Lowell's tenure. He adamantly pursued the quota policy, attempting in a variety of ways to defeat or circumvent the opposing faction. The preparatory "feeder" schools which supplied a considerable percentage of boys to the student bodies of the Big Three admitted few Jews, who were not welcome in the houses which domiciled and fed the resident students, the Protestant elite.[5]

The Big Three were important in this matter as examples of leadership training for the empire. Harvard President James Bryant Conant once referred to admissions policy as an "imperial life line."[6] Jews would come from public high schools and commute to the campus, which contributed to their isolation from student life, deemed so vital a feature of the educational process. This, of course, was the case at Princeton and Yale, as well as Harvard.

At Yale, few Jews had achieved faculty positions and those few mainly in the professional schools. None were tenured in the college before 1940. Social discrimination was the rule. Edward Sapir, world renowned Sterling Professor of Anthropology and Linguistics, was refused membership in the prestigious Graduate Club.

Ironically, unlike Harvard, Yale did not ask applicants' race and religion on admission forms until 1934, the year after the Nazi takeover.[7] The percentage of Jews in the class of 1933 was 8.2 percent, down from 13.3 percent in 1927.[8] President James R. Angell declined an invitation to address a mass meeting in New Háven in 1933 to protest "anti-Semitic excesses" in Germany, but denounced the loss of academic freedom in German universities while simultaneously hesitating to hire refugee scholars.[9]

Princeton appointed a few Jews to faculty positions in the mid-twenties. In 1940, in a class of 635 students, there were seventeen Jews.[10]

The reasons given by those advocating restrictions on the admission of Jewish students to determine and justify the discriminatory policies were based on the characteristics of Jews as perceived by the gentile elite. We find words like "unassimilated," "too studious," "untrustworthy," "Not ready." Scholastic criteria for admission were not applicable here. Jews ranked high academically and had to be excluded on other grounds.

President Lowell, in a letter to Professor William A. Hocking, May 19, 1922, urging a percentage system, held that:

> ... any group of men who did not mingle with the general stream—let us say Orientals, colored men, and perhaps French Canadians, if they did not speak English and kept themselves apart; or we might limit them by making the fact that men do not so mingle one of the causes of rejection above a certain percentage. This would apply to almost all but not all Jews; possibly, but not probably, to other people.[11]

Assimilation was also much on the minds of Jews who had "made it." Harry Wolfson, a Lithuanian-Jewish assistant professor of Jewish literature and philosophy, arguing in 1922 against the proposed restrictions to a group of its proponents, wrote:

> You assume assimilation is not complete until no two Jews are ever seen to walk together in the College Yard, and that the assimilation of Jews beyond a certain percentage is impossible. I say that all this should be made a subject of thorough study and investigation.[12]

Harvard's President Lowell had agreed to "take the best scholars ... irrespective of their social backgrounds," admitting not just the "sons of rich Jews."[13] In 1926 the chairman of Harvard's Admission Committee decided that they were "going to reduce their 25 percent

Hebrew total to 15 percent or less by simply rejecting without detailed explanation."[14] Harvard was singled out in the press for being "not the first, but merely the frankest" in announcing its restrictive admission policies.

The presentation of some salient features in the story of academic restrictions of Jews is vital to gaining a sense of the atmosphere the refugee scholars encountered when they tried to make contact in American academic institutions in the thirties. Lowell was troubled when he banned blacks from the freshman halls (at Harvard) and is quoted thus in confiding to his wife: "I wish I knew what our Savior would think it wise to do about the Negro in America."

Cambridge could make a Jew indistinguishable from an Anglo-Saxon Protestant, but not even Harvard could make a black man white.[15]

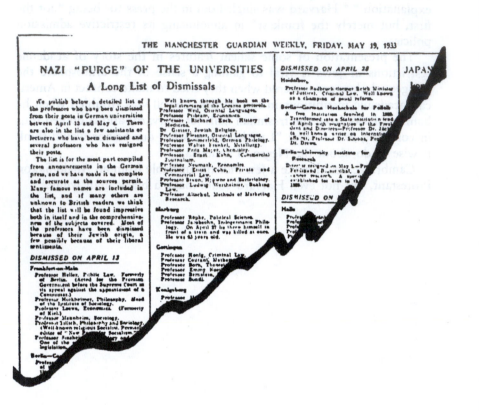

This May 1933 page from the venerable *Manchester Guardian* (U. K.) lends eloquent witness to the Nazis' determination to implement their program of "ethnic cleansing" and total control of all spheres of German life with the utmost dispatch. The first of these dismissals on this list were accomplished two and a half months after the takeover. I have included this document to show the extent of the threat confronting the victims so early, the totality of the action across the academic and geographic spectrum. It also proves once again that there was knowledge of the events inside Germany available to all the world with any interest in the dismal events enveloping Germany, from 1933.

THE MANCHESTER GUARDIAN WEEKLY, FRIDAY MAY 19, 1933

NAZI "PURGE" OF THE UNIVERSITIES

A Long List of Dismissals

We publish below a detailed list of the professors who have been dismissed from their posts in German universities between April 13 and May 4. There are also in the list a few assistants or lecturers who have been dismissed and several professors who have resigned their posts.

The list is for the most part compiled from announcements in the German press, and we have made it as complete and accurate as the sources permit. Many famous names are included in the list, and if many others are unknown to British readers we think that the list will be found impressive both in itself and in the comprehensiveness of the subjects covered. Most of the professors have been dismissed because of their Jewish origin, a few because of their liberal sentiments.

DISMISSED ON APRIL 13

Frankfurt-on-Main

Professor Heller, Public Law. Formerly of Berlin. (Acted for the Prussian Government before the Supreme Court in its appeal against the appointment of a Commissar.)

Professor Horkheimer, Philosophy. Head of the Institute of Sociology.

Professor Loewe, Economics. (Formerly of Kiel.)

Professor Mannheim, Sociology.

Professor Tillich, Philosophy and Sociology. (Well known religious Socialist. Formerly editor of "New Pages for Socialism.")

Professor Sinsheimer, Sociology and Law. One of the creators of German labour legislation.

Berlin—Commercial Hochschule

Professor Bonn, Economics. Twice Rector of the Hochschule. A Liberal. Sometimes referred to as "the German Keynes."

Berlin
   Professor Emil Lederer, Economics. (Formerly of Heidelberg. Editor
of the "Archiv fuer Sozialwissenschaft und Sozialpolitik.")

Breslau
   Professor Cohn.
   Professor Marck, Philosophy of Law.

Halle
   Professor Dehn, Practical Theology.

Koenigsberg—Commercial Hochschule
   Professor Feiler, Economics. A Liberal, Well known through his books
on U.S.A. and Russia. Formerly editor of the "Frankfurter Zeitung."

Bonn
   Professor Kantorowicz, Dentistry.
   Professor Loewenstein, Psychiatry.

Kiel
   Professor Kantotowics, Criminal Law.

Cologne
   Professor Kelsen, Public Law. (Formerly of Vienna, where he collaborated in the drafting of the Austrian Constitution. One of Germany's
greatest constitutional lawyers. A Liberal.)

Heidelberg
   Professor Hans von Eckardt. Principal the Institute of Journalism.

Dresden—Art Academy
   Professor Otto Dix, Teacher. (Not under Civil Service Law, but on
the ground that some of his pictures offended against morality. Others
were calculated to lessen the German people's will to defend itself
(Wehrwille). His famous picture "War," a huge oil-painting, represents
the horrors of modern warfare.)

Goettingen
Resigned in protest on April 18—Professor James Franck, Experimental Physics. Nobel Priseman, 1925. (As a war veteran not affected by the Civil Service law.)

Heidelberg
Professor Gerhard Anschutz, Public Law (resigned on April 22). One of the greatest German authorities on international law.
Professor Alfred Weber, Sociology (resigned on April 22).

DISMISSED ON APRIL 22

Hanover—Technical Hochschule
Professor Lessing, Philosophy (from lecture courses).

Berlin—Technical Hochschule
Professor Chajes, Industrial Hygiene (from lecture courses).
Professor Holde, Chemistry (from lecture courses).
Professor Fritz Frank, Chemical Research.
Professor Igel, Railway Construction.

DISMISSED ON APRIL 26

Frankfurt-on-Main
Professor Salomon, Sociology.
Professor Mennicke.
Professor M. Wertheimer, Psychology.
Professor Strupp, International Law. Well known through his book on the legal structure of the Locarno protocols.
Professor Weil, Oriental Languages.
Professor Pribram, Economics.
Professor Richard Koch, History of Medicine.
Professor Glatzer, Jewish Religion.
Professor Plessner, Oriental Languages.
Professor Sommerfeld, German Philology.
Professor Walter Frankel, Metallurgy.
Professor Fritz Mayer, Chemistry.
Professor Ernst Kahn, Commercial Journalism.

Professor Neumark, Economics.
Professor Ernst Cohn, Private and Commercial Law.
Professor Braun, Hygiene and Bacteriology.
Professor Ludwig Wertheimer, Banking Law.
Professor Altschul, Methods of Marketing Research.

Marburg
Professor Ropke, Political Science
Professor Jakobsohn, Indogermanic Philology. On April 27 he threw himself in front of a train and was killed at once. He was 53 years old.

Goettingen
Professor Honig, Criminal Law.
Professor Courant, Mathematics.
Professor Born, Theoretical Physics.
Professor Emmy Noether.
Professor Bernstein, Statistics.
Professor Bondi.

Koenigsbrg
Professor Hensel, Public Law (may be reappointed).

Koenigsberg—Commercial Hochschule
Professor Rogowsky, Practical Economis.
Professor Hansler.
Professor Kurba.

Kiel
Professor Colm, Economics.
Professor Neisser, Economics.
Professor Adolf Frankel, Mathematics.
Professor Husserl, Roman Law.
Professor Stenzel, Philosophy.
Professor Liepe, Modern German Philology and Literature.
Professor Rauch.
Professor Schucking, International Law. The chief German exponent of the legal conceptions on which the League of Nations is based. Has represented Germany at the Hague Court.
Professor Opet, German Law.

Berlin-Schoeneberg—State Art School
  Professor Georg Tappert.
  Professor Curt Labs.
  Lehrer Joseph Vinecky.

Berlin—Combined State Schools for Free and Applied Art
  Professor Karl Hofer. One of the greatest of modern German painters.
  Professor Edwin Scharff.

Duesseldorf Art Academy
  Professor Paul Klee. One of the pioneers of "expressionism." Well
known in Paris and London.
  Professor Oskar Moll, Director.

DISMISSED ON APRIL 27

Berlin—Hochschule fuer Music
  Professor Dr. Daniel
  Professor Kreutzer.
  Professor Feuermann.
  Professor Iloerth.
  Professor Dr. Schuenemann, Director.

Koenigsberg
  Professor Paneth, Chemistry.
  Professor Reidemeister, Mathematics.

Elbing
  Professor Otto Haase, Director.
  Professor Dr. Karl Thieme.
  Professor Hans Haffenrichter.
  Professor Emil Gossow.
  Professor Frau Helene Ziegert.
  Dosent Johannes Kretschmann.

Halle
  Professor Dr. Julius Frankenberger, Director.
  Professor Frau Anna Dernehl.
  Professor Martin Rang.

Professor Herbert Kranz.
Professor Dr. Adolf Reichwein.
Professor Dr. Karl von Hollander.
Professor Fritz Kauffmann.
Professor Dr. Hans Hoffmann.

Kiel
Professor Dr. Emil Fuchs.
Professor Wilhelm Oppermann.
Dosent Dr. Friedrich Copel.

Dortmund
Professor Johannes Sippel.
Dosent Dr. Hans Pflug.
Dosent Dr. Conrad Ameln.

Frankfurt-on-Main
Professor Martin Schmidt.
Professor Frau Dr. Marie Anne Kuntze.
Professor Frau Dr. Gerda Simons.
Professor Dr. Hermann Semiller.
Professor Dr. Friefrich Wilhelm Spemann.
Professor Hans Thierbach.
Dosent Frau Berta Kieser.

Bonn
Professor Hans Rosenberg.

DISMISSED ON APRIL 28

Heidelberg
Professor (former Reich Minister of Justice). Criminal Law. Well
known as a champion of penal reform.

Berlin—German Hochschule fuer Politik.
A free institution founded in 1920. Transformed into a State institu-
tion (end of April) with resignation of the President and Directors—
Professor Dr. Jackh (a well known writer on international affairs.
Professor Dr. Simons, Professor Dr. Drews.

Berlin—University Institute for Cancer Research.
Director resigned on May 1.—Professor Dr. Ferdinand Blumenthal, a pioneer of cancer research. A special chair was established for him in his subject in 1929.

DISMISSED ON MAY 1

Halle
Professor Fraenkl, History of Art.
Professor Kisch, History of German Law.
Professor Kitsinger, Criminal Law.
Professor Utitz, Philosophy.
Professor Hertz, Sociology (Viennese by birth, and now in Vienna. He wrote as a young man a well known book, "Moderne Rassentheorien," opposing the theories of Stewart Houston Chamberlin).
Professor Dozent Dr. Baer, Pure Mathematics.

DISMISSED ON MAY 2

Berlin
Professor Dr. Peter Roua, Colloid Chemistry and Physiology.
Professor Dr. Friedrich Franz Friedmann, Tubercular Research.
Professor Dr. Hans Friedenthal, Physiology.
Professor Dr. Hans Blumenthal, Dermatology.
Professor Dr. Birnbaum, Psychiatry.
Professor Dr. Mittwoch, Semitic Philology.
Professor Dr. Julius Pokorny, Celtic Philology, author of studies of the culture and literature of Ireland.
Professor Dr. Issai Schur, Mathematics. One of the leading mathematicians in Germany.
Professor Dr. Manes, Insurance.
Professor Dr. Byk, Quantum Theory of Physics.
Professor Dr. Fischel, History of Art.
Professor Dr. Jollos, Zoology.
Professor Dr. Walter Norden, Municipal Administration.
Professor Dr. Richter, Medicine.
Professor Dr. Hans Pringsheim, Chemistry.
Professor Dr. Hermann Grossmann, Technology.

Dosent Dr. Otto Linemann (?), Applied Psychology.
Dosent Dr. Konrad Cohn Dentistry.

Deprived of their Lecture Courses
Dosent Dr. Fritz Baade, a Socialist. Authority on agrarian questions.
Dosent Dr. Balogh.
Dosent Dr. Kurt Haentzschel, Press Law.
Dosent Dr. Wakter Lands.
Professor Dr. Wolf Eisner, Medicine.

Cologne
Professor Schmalenbach, Economics.
Professor Schmittmann, Economics (arrested May 3 on charges of Separatist activity).
Professor Spitzer.
Professor Cohn-Vossen, Mathematics.
Professor Braunfels.
Professor Lips, Sociology.
Professor Esch, Communications.
Professor Beyer, Industrial and Technical Pedagogy.
Professor Honigsheim, Philosophy and Sociology.

Jena
Professor Emil Klein, Medicine.
Professor Theodor Meyer-Steinegg, History of Medicine.
Professor Hans Stimmel.
Professor Mathilde Vaerting, Theory of Education.
Professor Dr. Wilhelm Peters, Psychology (at own request).
Professor Schazel, Zoology.
Professor Berthold Josephy, Economic and Social Sciences.
Privat Dozent Leo Brauner, Botany.

Aachen—Technical Hochschule
Professor Hopf, Higher Mathematics.
Professor Fuchs.
Professor Meusel, Economics.
Professor Mautner, Iron Construction.
Professor Levy, Organic Chemistry.

Privat Dozent Strauss, Literature.
Privat Dozent Pick.

DISMISSED ON MAY 3

Berlin—Technical Hochschule
Professor Dr. Kurrein, Technical Research.
Professor Dr. Schlesinger, Industrial Machinery.
Professor Dr. Schwerin, Theory of Elasticity.
Professor Dr. Levy, Economics.
Professor Dr. Lehmann, Photographic Chemistry.
Professor Korn, Photo-telegraphy.
Professor Traube, Colloid Chemistry.
Professor Salinger, Low tension Electricity Technique.
Privat Dozent Dr. Kelen, Hydraulic Structures.
Herr Grabowski, Lecturer.

Greifswald
Professor Klingmueller, Roman and Private Law.
Professor Ziegler, Classical Philology.

Munster
Professor Freud.
Professor Bruck, Economics.
Professor Heilbronn, Botany.

Berlin
Professor James Goldschmidt, Criminal Law (resigned).
Professor Fritz Haber, Physical Chemistry, Nobelpriseman (Inventor of the synthetic ammonia manufacturing process on which Germany depended during the world war. It has been said that but for him Germany would have had to capitulate early in the war.)
Professor Freundlich, Colloid Chemistry (resigned).
Professor Polanyi, Physical Chemistry (resigned).
Professor Spranger, Philosophy and Pedagogy (resigned).

Berlin—Agricultural Hochschule
Professor Dr. Karl Brandt, Agricultural Marketing Research.

DISMISSED MAY 4

Leipzig
  Professor Witkowski, Literary History (A noted student of Goethe).
  Professor Walter Goetz, History. (One of the foremost German historians. Editor of the Propylaen Weltgeschichte. Democratic member of the Reichstag 1920–1928).
  Professor Apelt, Public Law. (Formerly Saxon Minister of the Interior.)
  Professor Everth, Journalism.
  Professor Hellmann, Medical History.
  Privat Dozent Dr. Becker.

Dresden—Technical Hochschule
  Professor Dr. Holldack, Law.

Leipzig—Teachers' Training College
  Professor Dr. Johannes Richter (Principal).

NOTES

1. Reinhard Rurup, *"Emanzipation und Antisemitismas"* (Goettingen: Vandenhoeck & Ruprecht, 1975), p. 29.
2. Ploetz, *Das Deutsche Kaiserreich* (Freiburg: Verlag Ploetz, 1984), p. 147.
3. Norbert Kampe: *Studenten und Judenfrage im Deutschen Kaiserreich* (Goettingen: Vandenhoeck & Ruprecht, 1988), p. 80.
4. David Levering Lewis, "Parallels and Divergences: Assimilationist Strategies of Afro-American and Jewish Elites from 1910 to the Early 1930s," *Journal of American History*, Vol. 71, No. 3 (December 1984), p. 548.
5. Marcia Graham Synott, *The Half-Opened Door* (Westport, Conn.: Greenwood Press, 1979), p. 12.
6. Ibid., p. 5.
7. Ibid., p. 155.
8. Ibid., pp. 157–158.
9. Ibid., pp. 156–157.
10. Ibid., p. 195.
11. Ibid., p. 21.
12. Ibid., p. 67.
13. Ibid.
14. Ibid., p. 110.
15. Bruce Kuklick, *The Rise of American Philosophy* (New Haven: Yale University Press, 1977), p. 407.

CHAPTER 2

"Twenty Thousand Charming Children Would All Too Soon Grow into 20,000 Ugly Adults."

It is clear from the preceding pages that the reception the displaced scholars were to receive in the academic establishment was ambivalent. On the one hand, they were welcomed, depending on their perceived scholarly distinctions, as harbingers of much revered European culture and achievement. There exists a fair amount of literature on the luminaries who were immediately in demand and established in the most prestigious schools. Even the less famous exiles, with some credentials or reputations among their American colleagues, were afforded respect and given opportunities to resume their interrupted careers, and lives, in their chosen fields in "good" institutions. The situation demanded a selection process, best described in the internal correspondence among Rockefeller Foundation officers charged with the task of placing the scholars.

In a letter dated June 15, 1933, from Dr. Alan Gregg, Rockefeller Foundation director of Medical Sciences, to his colleagues:

> Categories of scholars to be aided: Distinguished scholars of established reputation (Class 1), and brilliant younger scholars of proved ability (Class II), the young men of promise (Class III), on the other hand, should be excluded.[1]

This very early scheme can be understood in light of the prevailing conviction that the situation in Germany was not really hopeless. Two months earlier, a letter on May 13, 1933, from Robert A. Lambert,

M. D., associate director to Dr. Alan Gregg, director, Rockefeller Foundation Medical Sciences, states:

> I believe it is the feeling of a majority of the group here (European office in Paris) that we ought not to proceed on the theory that exiled scholars would never return to Germany. Right now, I would be ready to bet that a good many will be invited back within a year.

In addition to these false hopes, there were the facts of the continuing severe depression in America with its widespread unemployment and increasing xenophobia, as well as anti-Semitism.

New York, May 26, 1933, Alan Gregg to colleagues:

> If too many Jews are introduced into American universities, we shall run a surprisingly good chance of creating an uncontrollable amount of precisely the same sort of illiberal attitude here. The men I talked to on this committee would prefer anything to fanning the flames of anti-Semitism on this side of the water.

The committee included Felix Warburg, Fred M. Stein, Bernard Flexner, Alfred Cohen, Stephen Duggan, the director of the Emergency Committee. All but Duggan were Jews. While it is true that it was originally the East European Jews who were the target of the prejudicial policies, at the time of the influx of the German Jewish refugees, this factor does not seem to have played a role anymore. Understandably, fear of displacing American faculty and exacerbating unemployment were potent elements in those hard times. A letter to the Emergency Committee from March 1936 reads:

> The Emergency Committee continues to feel that the criterion of the Rockefeller Foundation, which it shares, i.e., to aid men assured of permanent positions, is the only satisfactory way for it to operate. The Emergency Committee is resolutely against aiding the younger group of deposed Germans, since, as Bernard Flexner says, there is a large enough number of young American scholars without positions.

Perhaps the most notorious and widely publicized examples of virulent anti-Semitic organized groups of the thirties were the followers of the "radio priest," Father Coughlin, of the Shrine of the Little Flower in Royal Oak, Michigan. He began broadcasting sermons in the early

1930s to experiment with the new medium of radio. By the early years of the New Deal, he had launched increasingly vitriolic attacks on Franklin Roosevelt, Wall Street, communism and the Jews. He gained a large audience until 1942, when the war and the Catholic hierarchy put a stop to his broadcasts and his magazine, *Social Justice.*[2]

Then there was the emerging German American Bund, an outright Nazi military organization, complete with brown uniforms, swastika armbands and several camps where military drill was practiced. By 1939 its membership was about 20,000, mostly American citizens of German descent. The Bund disintegrated with the U.S. entry into the war. It had received covert financial support and guidance from the Nazi government.

The Ku Klux Klan claimed a membership of over 100,000 in 1930, with Jews, Catholics, and blacks their target of abuse. There were other similar hate groups, but all of these were rather marginal to mainstream American society. Nevertheless, in 1938, a confidential poll by the Opinion Research Corporation found that 82 percent of those polled were opposed to large-scale immigration of German Jews.[3]

Understandably, Roosevelt was sensitive to these findings and thus not disposed toward increasing the quota or taking other steps to ease the immigration of refugees or the requirements necessary to obtain visas. Congress was totally opposed to increasing immigration or allowing more refugees into the country under special legislation. A plan to bring 20,000 Jewish children from Austria and Germany into the United States by this means was not implemented. The wife of immigration commissioner James Houghteling, Laura Delano, FDR's first cousin, advised against the bill: "Twenty-thousand charming children would all too soon grow into 20,000 ugly adults."[4]

Few State Department officials favored increased refugee immigration. A remarkably prescient exception was Raymond Geist, consul in Berlin, who prophesied in December 1938: "The Jews in Germany are being condemned to death and their sentence will be slowly carried out; but probably too fast for the world to save them."[5]

Sentiments of xenophobia and anti-Semitism accompanied the competition for scarce jobs. These circumstances led Jewish leaders and organizations to feel fearful of inflaming anti-Semitic sentiments and were inhibiting factors in their steady activities on behalf of their increasingly imperiled co-religionists in Europe.

The famous research institution in Berlin, the Kaiser Wilhelm Institute, heavily supported by the Rockefeller Foundation, was from the beginning of Nazi rule a source of a number of deposed scholars and thus a focus of the Foundation's concern. The Foundation had made a major financial commitment in 1930 to the Institute and now found itself in the dilemma of honoring its commitment and supporting Nazi-directed research or reneging on its pledge.

There was much correspondence about this dilemma and, in the end, the funding was granted, in order not to renege on the commitment. A letter from Professor Felix Frankfurter, then at the Harvard Law School, not yet Supreme Court justice, wrote in response to a letter from Raymond B. Fosdick, president of the Rockefeller Foundation, dated December 9, 1936, in part:

> Making a gift to Nazi Germany in punctilious fulfillment of a pledge antedating the Nazi regime is one thing; justifying such a gift with the statement that "The world of science is a world without flags or frontiers" quite another. The letter means nothing unless it means that present-day Germany is a world in which the untainted and relevant criteria of science predominate. To imply that they do when they do not may quite uncolorfully be characterized as a tendency to "adulterate the spiritual coinage of the world."

Fosdick's letter had quoted an article on the subject in *The New York Times*.

It turned out that the funding was used to set up a laboratory which pursued chemical research for war-related aims. A report from the Kaiser Wilhelm Institute of June 15, 1934, quotes the eminent Jewish chemist, Dr. Otto Warburg (protected by the Nazis throughout), in a chat with an American visitor: "Warburg thinks that the worst of the Jew-baiting is probably past. No longer gives the impression of being troubled as he did in the past. . . . Rather pleased that his straight dealing with the Nazis has worked satisfactorily. Is not concerned apparently at developments in the immediate future of his own institute" (from Alan Gregg's diary).

One of the several survey trips to campuses in different parts of the United States was undertaken by Professor Walter Kotschnig, who reports from the University of California, Berkeley, that Carl Sauer, professor of geography, maintained in April 1936: "People would have to be first class, particularly if they are Jews." As late as November 6, 1940, a letter to *The New York Times* from "a Ph.D. from New Haven, Connecticut," asks: " . . . if the European scholar, who is at least part responsible for the collapse of his world must be preserved for scholarly endeavor. . . . " A thought-provoking notion, that.

I have included the foregoing quotes to give a sense of the times from 1933 to 1940. The continuing incredulity that Germany, a Christian, highly civilized bastion of European culture and learning, could sink into barbarism played a powerful role for some time. The reported outrages and tales of terror were deemed unfortunate aberrations, soon to be alleviated by more benevolent policies. The fact that terror was, in fact, Nazi policy was simply beyond the comprehension of most observers.

It must be kept in mind from the present perspective that anyone predicting the horrors Europe was to suffer between 1933 and 1945 would have been diagnosed as paranoid. The view that Hitler's Germany was to be a short-lived phenomenon, soon to be replaced by "saner elements," variously identified, was to remain accepted wisdom in important decision-making bodies, until the annexation of Austria in March 1938, the *Anschluss*, and the subsequent reign of terror on the 9th of November, known as *Kristallnacht*, for the widespread smashing of Jewish homes and stores and the resulting piles of broken glass on the street. Hundreds of homes, many synagogues and some 7,000 Jewish businesses were destroyed. More than 900 Jews were killed and thousands of people terrorized, beaten, arrested, and dispossessed.[6]

Nineteen-thirty-eight then saw the beginning of the increasing sense of urgency on the part of the individuals and organizations which had taken on the task of bringing people out of Germany, and then Austria, which meant securing visas, means of transport, and, in our study, securing livelihoods and, preferably, teaching positions for the scholars.

The generations whose personal memory does not embrace this history have to engage in a leap of the imagination to grasp and confront those times. Unlived history remains abstraction absent a conscious act of will and the imaginative intelligence. This applies to the American experience with respect to the history of slavery and the continuing racism Americans still struggle with. Obviously, all nation-states have dreadful episodes in their experience, and the same imperatives apply to all, lest the ghosts persist to haunt.

The Rockefeller Foundation continued its support work throughout

World War II, as developments affecting the scholars' situations deteriorated ever more rapidly with the spread of the German conquests and the occupation of most European countries. Another key organization in these efforts was the Emergency Rescue Committee in Aid of Displaced Foreign Scholars, central for our focus.

As a nation of immigrants, there were numerous organizations already in place to aid newly arrived Jews experienced in the necessary tasks, such as securing housing and other means of survival during the first period of settling-in for those without supportive relatives. New organizations were established to address the needs of this group of refugees, different in culture, language, education and class than earlier immigrants from Central and Eastern Europe and, later, from Western Europe, as well.

Aside from the Emergency Committee, there was Alvin Johnson's University in Exile at the very centrally involved New School for Social Research, and, after 1936, the Self-Help of German Refugees. There were others as well, including the American Friends Service Committee, and more short-lived groups, less essential in the areas which are the subject of this investigation.

As of 1938, the following organizations were listed on the letterhead of the National Coordinating Committee for Aid to Refugees and Emigrants Coming from Germany:

American Committee for Christian-German Refugees
American Friends Service Committee
American Jewish Committee
American Jewish Congress
American Joint Distribution Committee
Committee for Catholic Refugees from Germany
Emergency Committee in Aid of Displaced German Physicians
Emergency Committee in Aid of Displaced German Scholars
Federal Council of Churches of Christ in America
German-Jewish Children's Aid, Inc.
Hebrew Sheltering and Immigrant Aid Society
Hospites
Independent Order of B'nai B'rith
International Migration Service
International Student Service
Musicians Emergency Fund, Inc.
National Council of Jewish Federations and Welfare Funds
National Council of Jewish Women
Zionist Organization of America

Initially, the newly arrived in New York City were close to destitute; it was a capital crime to take more than ten marks per person out of Germany. Few had funds outside, also illegal. A number had relatives who supplied the prized affidavits, essential for the required immigration visa. These relatives had to meet the refugees at the boat and could frequently be counted on for housing and other immediate survival needs. Soon, most refugees visited the organizations which were attempting to place and settle people into some type of subsistence situation during their initial period of learning English and getting oriented in a strange new world.

Menial work in households, restaurants, shops and factories was usually the source of the first paycheck. At the same time, the priorities were learning English and exploring the possibilities for work which was more in accord with skills and former occupations. In many families, it was the women who found jobs more easily in traditional women's work: cooking, cleaning, child care, sewing. It was less demeaning for them than their professor or lawyer husbands who, nevertheless, found themselves washing dishes in strange kitchens. The imperative was the language and the professional preparations, making contacts in their fields of work, where possible. Physicians had to pass language and basic sciences state exams. Lawyers had to start over in law school or find other occupations, as English common law, basic in the United States, was not the basis for continental law; Roman law, not taught in the United States, played that part.

It was also the case that women were far more likely to have studied English in school than men because the high schools likely to have been their choices taught modern languages, whereas the university preparatory high schools, the *Gymnasium*, emphasized Latin, Greek, and French. Moreover, young girls were sometimes sent to spend some months with a family in France or England to enhance a girl's education, social graces, and worldly experience.

In February 1938, the National Coordination Committee for Aid to Refugees and Emigrants Coming from Germany sent the following letter to presidents of "leading" colleges and universities.

Dear . . .

One of the leading Foundations in the country has recently issued a Confidential List of Displaced German Scholars—men and women who have rendered distinguished service in Germany in the fields of Archeology, Biology, Chemistry, Engineering, Law, Mathematics, Philosophy, Medicine, the Social and Economic Sciences. In fact, there is hardly a branch of intellectual activity which is not represented by distinguished men and women forced to leave Germany on account of social, political and religious oppression.

From time to time these refugees come to us for advice and guidance. They are eager to obtain academic positions. Those already placed in various colleges and universities throughout the country are giving a most satisfactory account of themselves. In the University-in-Exile, connected with the New School for Social Research (in New York) Displaced German Scholars are making notable contributions in the field of the Social and Economic Sciences.

Should your institution require the services of someone on any of your faculties, we hope you will write us and we will cheerfully send you the curriculum vitae of such a scholar.

With assurance of appreciation,
Cordially yours,
Jacob Billikopf

As the situation in Europe deteriorated with increasing Nazi power and decreasing hope for a speedy end to its domination, efforts to place the displaced were expanded and new avenues were sought. In a memo from the Rockefeller Foundation's Paris office to New York, March 15, 1938, three days after the Austrian takeover, we read:

... instead of the one percent in Germany, there will be 6 to 8 percent (Jewish scientists) in Austria. The world has absorbed emigres until it seems to me it has reached almost the saturation point, so that if we stick to our usual rules, there is going to be very little that we can do to help these people when they descend upon us. I assume that the Foundation will not again make an emergency program and I would not think we would be justified in making exception to our present rule of assisting only those outstanding people who are shortly to be absorbed in other institutions.

With the knowledge of the desperate situation abroad, the above attitude, or policy, seems inconsistent with increasing insight and intensified effort to place the emigres. The apparent contradiction, however, actually accords with the prevalent confusion and ambivalence about the looming catastrophe in Europe. It simply did not seem possible that the nightmare would not go away.

A Rockefeller Foundation report on its Special Aid Fund for Deposed Scholars 1933–39 reads:

> The displacement of scholars for political and racial reasons began in Germany in 1933. Subsequently, it has spread to Spain, Italy, Austria, Czechoslovakia, and now Poland. There are no accurate estimates of the extent of this disturbance. Every bit of evidence, however, strengthens the conclusion that as a mass migration of scholarly personnel, it is unprecedented in academic history.

After mentioning the occasional unsatisfactory placement in terms of the refugees' language or personality problems, it concludes:

> On the whole, the Foundation's program has been surprisingly successful. Academic departments and even whole institutions have been revitalized. There seems no doubt that the emigre scholars placed in our universities have made a distinctive and important contribution to the cultural life of America.

There is a postscript in a letter of September 24, 1938, from Friends of Refugee Teachers to the Emergency Committee:

> We also have now an application for a partial non-Aryan from a school whose head feels that they are more in need than full Jews. Have you anyone in this category?

This investigator has found no evidence that the organizations which attempted to place the displaced scholars ever made a point of differentiating their clients ethnically by religion.

In surveying the correspondence among the aid groups, hardly a word passed about the more than 100 historically black colleges in the United States. Mention is made, however, of the possibilities in Latin America and South Africa and contacts with those embassies are referred to. The reasons for this lack of contact with black colleges will be addressed in a subsequent chapter. There was a refugee in a black college as early as 1934, but there has been no document found to reveal how that contact was made. The college was Lemoyne-Owen in Memphis, Tennessee, not likely to have been addressed by the refugee aid organizations.

The first instance of direct, systematic effort I have identified is a

letter dated September 18, 1941, from the Emergency Committee to six
of the better known institutions: Fisk, Hampton, Shaw, Talladega, Spelman, Tuskegee, Bennett. It is addressed to the presidents of the respective colleges:

Dear President . . .

From some institutions the reports indicate that the enrollment is going
to be better than expected, and they inquire about displaced foreign scholars to supplement and widen the acquaintance of their campus community. The candidates we suggest have suffered from Nazi policies,
appreciate the relative freedom and democracy of the United States, and
have taken out their first papers or are already American citizens. They
are of Austrian, Czech, Danish, Polish and other nationalities as well as
German. Some have had teaching experience in the United States or have
been members of the American Seminars held by the Friends in summer,
where they have improved their English and oriented themselves to our
American community ideas and practice.

Beside those competent in the usual disciplines of the sciences and
mathematics, economics, sociology, history, education, history of music
and painting. There are scholars with fields of rarer interest. Two of our
candidates are especially interested in colored youth and would like to
discover opportunities to teach in colleges or schools with negro clientele.
Another is a teacher of drama and the dance whose ability has already
been demonstrated with a group of American youth, using music selected
from the "times of Washington". He has published a volume on the
history of the dance. In a small Pennsylvania college, through cooperation
between administration and faculty, a stipend was raised. An invitation
to a 'Visiting Lectureship' was cabled to Vichy and a Nobel Prize winning
French scholar may thus be saved from concentration camp.

Our new "Professional Development and Visiting Scholar Service" is
helping a member of a Spanish department to enjoy leave in 1941–1942
for professional development, while a displaced professor from Spain's
University of Valencia takes her place. If you would care to learn details
of this plan, I shall be glad to forward a statement of them to you.

With best wishes for the coming year, I am

Sincerely yours,
Laurence R. Seelye

There were some inquiries from church-related Southern colleges regarding the refugees' religious affiliations, but none has surfaced as a
condition for employment. There have been statements that Jewish faculty faithfully attended chapel in colleges with required attendance on
Sundays. In this connection, it is useful to understand that few of these

scholars were particularly observant religiously. There is an amusing and instructive comment on the part of a colleague at Talladega College to the effect that, "Pappenheim was not enough of a Jew," a reference to the absence of piety. In any case, Professor Pappenheim did attend chapel.

A revealing and extraordinary interoffice correspondence item from the Rockefeller Foundation of June 3, 1940, from Joseph H. Willits, Director, Social Science Division:

Subject: If Hitler wins —

The contours of the Europe which will result in case of a Nazi victory may now be reasonably clearly estimated, at least so far as Great Britain and France are concerned. There may be an attempt at total enslavement by incorporation into the Reich,— in which case concentration camps and executions for persons with capacity for independent leadership may be expected.

But even if a more "moderate" program is followed, the devastating consequences on life in France and Britain,—and on other defeated countries — are obvious. No one can predict the exact lines of Nazi policy, but such acts as these are likely elements in their picture if they conquer:

The amputation of most of the British and French Empires.

The compulsory adjustment of financial production and foreign trade policies to fit in with and serve the needs and greater prosperity of the German economic (military) system.

The forced migration of millions of people from their present homes and occupations in order to make room for expansion of the German race.

The suppression of all independent expression which is in any way critical of the acts or ideologies of the Nazi regime.

What these measures mean is clear,—both economically and intellectually. If, for example, Great Britain is forced to work on lines of production acceptable to Germany, is shut out of much of her European and Asiatic markets and much of her colonial markets, loses most of her international shipping business and her functions as international banker,—it may well be that Great Britain will not be able to support more than half the present population at the present standard of living. The resultant discontent will be perfect for Nazi purposes.

The intellectual consequences are no less appalling. Great Britain, France, Holland, Belgium, Denmark, Sweden, Switzerland, will almost certainly cease to offer the kind of milieu in which social science research can flourish.

With millions of people having to or desiring to migrate from their homelands, the pressure on the Foundation to become a relief body will be terrific. I suggest,—at least as far as SS (Social Science) is concerned,—that we choose now as the small part of the total task which the Foundation's limited resources permit it to undertake, the responsibility for relocating such of the best of the scientific and scholarly men and women from France, Great Britain and other over-run countries as may be available to leave.

I would suggest these fundamental departures from the refugee policies which have obtained in the past:

1. I would take the initiative and shop for the best. I would do this cold-bloodedly on the assumption that Nazi domination of these countries makes them a poor place for a first-class person to remain in. And on the further assumption that the Foundation could make no finer contribution to our culture than to bring over, say, 100 of the best minds from Great Britian, 75 from France, and smaller numbers from the other countries. We could contribute to much needed distinction of our universities by facilitating such immigration.

In the case of the German refugees, we waited for what the individuals concerned were able to promote or universities originated. I think it is not unfair to say that a great many were not really first-rate.

In reversing this process I would suggest that we start now with the collaboration of a few leading social scientists in considering the idea. If the plan were approved, a list of the men and women in the various social science fields whom we would most like to see here could be prepared. Thus we could be ready if the final tragedy occurs. This should be done as quietly as possible. Such a list should not be used woodenly, and of course we could and would lower the standard to fit many situations; but the emphasis should be on the highest quality. Most of the others would just have to turn to other perhaps less intellectual occupations.

2. I would consider that all North America,—especially Canada,—and all South and Central America would constitute possible markets for these scholars. We have been searching for "something to do" in South America. I think this could be one concrete way to begin.

3. If this policy were adopted, we would be immediately confronted with the "elbows out" attitude toward refugees on many United States campuses. I think this difficulty need not be insurmountable. The emotional attitude in the event of Nazi victory will be different. Concentration on high quality will also help. Furthermore, English and French scholars will be more readily fitted into the American scene than have some of the German refugees. And finally, it may be necessary to increase the rate and period of Foundation support.

RF spent $750,000 in assisting refugees, chiefly from Germany, to locate in this country. It may be confronted with an opportunity,—greater for the United States and greater for civilization.

Two steps would seem to be necessary to implement this policy:

1. Quietly, with a few leading scholars, explore this plan and, if approved, develop the list of preferred scholars.

2. Be prepared for systematic exploration of the market and quick action if necessary.

If Hitler loses —
    Then the need will be of a totally different character,—with prompt action
of a totally different kind indicated.

By 1940, as the war in Europe loomed ever closer in the minds of
Washington policymakers, their concern over the refugees' constituting
a "Fifth Column" by infiltrating saboteurs, spies, and other subversives,
generated concrete policy measures. This kind of subversion was suspected to have been a contributing factor in the fall of France and
confirmed the administration's convictions that immigration must be
increasingly restricted and that an eye must be kept on aliens in the
country. Congress passed the Smith Act in June 1940, requiring all
aliens to be registered and fingerprinted. Members of fascist or communist organizations were to be deported and the advocacy of the violent overthrow of the government was made a crime.

Also in 1940–41, the aid organizations in the United States explored
opportunities for refugee scholars in the West, Midwest and South by
sending emissaries to colleges in those areas. No mention is made in
the reports of black colleges.

The American Friends Service Committee issued a report to the Emergency Committee on an "informal field study" by their education counsellor, which covered fifty-six colleges and interviewed "about 140
college presidents, deans, registrars, heads of departments, etc." The
counsellor reports sympathy for refugees, budgetary restrictions, a desire
for more Ph.Ds. and the possibilities of acquiring personnel for little
money. The difficulties listed included language problems, anti-German
sentiment, nativist American conservatism concerning alien methods
and the substance of teaching. Little anti-Semitic feeling is found, but
professing Christians are desirable in church-related colleges. The following passages are of interest:

> From two points of view there is considerable danger of exploitation in
> the absorption of foreign scholars into the American college system. Too
> many refugees have taken advantage of kindness, gained a foothold and
> have proven incompetent, or unworthy of their appointment. On the other
> hand, there is danger that colleges will exploit the foreign professor and
> occasion bitterness among American faculty by displacing well qualified
> Americans in getting services of the foreign born more cheaply.

The services provided by the Refugee Section were outlined. First, the clearing house and nominations from the group of qualified and successful teachers who are equipped for assuming full responsibility at once, and second, a similar list of nominees who need a period of adaptation. It was explained that members of the latter group are willing to become interns and work in a subordinate capacity while improving their use of English and learning American teaching methods. This group contains many holders of Ph.D. degrees who are content to receive maintenance and small compensation in return for full time services on a lower level. They are especially useful in relieving those departments where temporary over-registration often proves embarrassing. They are often versatile enough to assist in this way in more than one department.

This trip covered colleges in the South. There is no mention in the report of historically black colleges. It is therefore difficult to know if these were included in the study.

From Harvard University, we have a letter of October 4, 1940, from an official to the Emergency Committee which reports on a conversation with President Conant about prospects for refugees at Harvard. Aside from more practical considerations such as space, willingness of departments to have them and time limits, the following reservation was communicated:

> Apart from the scholarly competence and personal acceptability of the refugee scholars, the reasonable limitation of their number as members of the University community have to be considered.

The category at issue here was funded by the Rockefeller Foundation, not by Harvard. Another factor mentioned in this same letter is:

> ... the very large number of foreigners who have come into residence in the University, in one capacity or another, including, but very greatly exceeding, the category to which I have referred. We do not think that the number should be materially enlarged.

The category mentioned are the "Research Fellow by Special Appointment," seven or eight, funded by "special sources."

In a memo, "Suggestions for Development of the Emergency Committee Field Program 1941–42," we note the listing of eight items under "In General Strengthen these Incentives in Colleges":

1. Desire to help able scholars who are in need.

2. Desire to offer DFS opportunities to become better prepared for further teaching in the U.S.A.

3. Desire to import unusual intellectual or social influences to the campus.

4. Desire to supplement or develop offerings in certain departments or to start new departments.

5. Respect for European scholarship and cultivation.

6. Desire to further research and the research spirit on the local campus.

7. Willingness, at a time of straitened income, to get "something for little."

8. Desire to enjoy opportunities conducive to the refreshment of local faculty minds: especially if the faculty have been long on campus in snug communities, with little chance for travel and for broad provocative acquaintance.

On December 11, 1941, four days after Japan's attack on Pearl Harbor, Germany and Japan declared war on the United States. Once a state of war existed, aliens became enemy aliens, and all citizenship proceedings were halted pending an FBI investigation and subsequent clearance from subversive activities. This was a period of great concern on the West Coast, as the evacuation and internment of Germans was considered by the federal government. But the Japanese were to be rounded up first, American citizens for the most part, who spent the rest of the war in internment camps, one of the more shameful chapters of the period.

It was decided to address the disposition of the Europeans after the Japanese evacuation was accomplished. Racism operating against the Japanese was certainly an additional factor here. This delay spared the Italians and the Germans the fate of the Japanese, in part also because a number of influential individuals and organizations interceded on the refugees' behalf. There were regulations issued for fingerprinting and photos for identity cards, possession of short-wave radios and carrying cameras were prohibited, as was leaving one's city of residence without the U.S. Attorney's permission. These regulations varied in different regions of the country.

BLACK COLLEGES

Name	Year Founded	Location
ALABAMA (12)		
Alabama A&M University	1875	Huntsville, AL 35762
Alabama State University	1874	Montgomery, AL 36195
S.D. Bishop State Jr. College	1936	Mobile, AL 36690
Concordia College	1922	Selma, AL 36701
Lawson State Community College	1949	Birmingham, AL 35221
Miles College	1905	Birmingham, AL 35208
Oakwood College	1896	Huntsville, AL 35896
Selma University	1878	Selma, AL 36701
Stillman College	1876	Tuscaloosa, AL 35403
Talladega College	1867	Talladega, AL 35160
Trenholm State Technical College	1963	Montgomery, AL 36108
Tuskegee University	1881	Tuskegee, AL 36088
ARKANSAS (4)		
Arkansas Baptist College	1884	Little Rock, AR 72202
Philander Smith College	1877	Little Rock, AR 72202
Shorter College	1886	N. Little Rock, AR 72114
University of Arkansas, Pine Bluff	1873	Pine Bluff, AR 71601
DELAWARE (1)		
Delaware State College	1891	Dover, DE 19901
DISTRICT OF COLUMBIA (2)		
Howard University	1867	Washington, DC 20059
University of the District of Columbia	1851	Washington, DC 20008
FLORIDA (4)		
Bethune-Cookman College	1904	Daytona Beach, FL 32015
Edward Waters College	1866	Jacksonville, FL 32209
Florida A&M University	1887	Tallahassee, FL 32307
Florida Memorial College	1879	Miami, FL 33054
GEORGIA (10)		
Albany State College	1903	Albany, GA 31705
Atlanta University	1865	Atlanta, GA 30314
Clark College	1869	Atlanta, GA 30314
Fort Valley State College	1895	Fort Valley, GA 31030
Morehouse College	1867	Atlanta, GA 30314
Morehouse School of Medicine	1981	Atlanta, GA 30310
Morris Brown College	1881	Atlanta, GA 30314

Paine College	1882	Augusta, GA 30910
Savannah State College	1890	Savannah, GA 31404
Spelman College	1881	Atlanta, GA 30314

KENTUCKY (2)

Kentucky State University	1886	Frankfort, KY 40601
Simmons University Bible College	1873	Louisville, KY 40210

LOUISIANA (6)

Dillard University	1869	New Orleans, LA 70122
Grambling State University	1901	Grambling, LA 71245
Southern University System	1974	Baton Rouge, LA 70813
Southern University at Baton Rouge	1880	Baton Rouge, LA 70813
Southern University at New Orleans	1956	New Orleans, LA 70126
Southern University at Shreveport	1964	Shreveport, LA 71107
Xavier University	1925	New Orleans, LA 70125

MARYLAND (4)

Bowie State College	1865	Bowie, MD 20715
Coppin State College	1900	Baltimore, MD 21216
Morgan State University	1867	Baltimore, MD 21239
University of Maryland, Eastern Shore	1886	Princess Anne, MD 21853

MISSISSIPPI (10)

Alcorn State University	1871	Lorman, MS 39096
Coahoma Jr. College	1949	Clarksdale, MS 38614
Jackson State University	1877	Jackson, MS 39217
Mary Holmes College	1892	West Point, MS 39773
Mississippi Valley State University	1950	Itta Bena, MS 38941
Natchez Jr. College	1885	Natchez, MS 39120
Prentiss Institute Jr. College	1907	Prentiss, MS 39474
Rust College	1866	Holly Springs, MS 38635
Tougaloo College	1869	Tougaloo, MS 39174
Utica Campus-Hinds Jr. College	1903	Utica, MS 39175

MISSOURI (2)

Harris-Stowe State College	1857	St. Louis, MO 63103
Lincoln University	1866	Jefferson City, MO 65101

NORTH CAROLINA (11)

Barber-Scotia College	1867	Concord, NC 28025
Bennett College	1873	Greensboro, NC 27402
Elizabeth City State University	1891	Elizabeth City, NC 27909
Fayetteville State University	1877	Fayetteville, NC 28301
Johnson C. Smith University	1867	Charlotte, NC 28216
Livingstone College	1879	Salisbury, NC 28144
North Carolina A&T State University	1891	Greensboro, NC 27411

Name	Year Founded	Location
North Carolina Central University	1910	Durham, NC 27707
Saint Augustine's College	1867	Raleigh, NC 27611
Shaw University	1865	Raleigh, NC 27611
Winston-Salem State University	1892	Winston-Salem, NC 27110
OHIO (2)		
Central State University	1887	Wilberforce, OH 45384
Wilberforce University	1856	Wilberforce, OH 45384
OKLAHOMA (1)		
Langston University	1897	Langston, OK 73050
PENNSYLVANIA (2)		
Cheyney University	1837	Cheyney, PA 19319
Lincoln University	1854	Lincoln University, PA 19352
SOUTH CAROLINA (8)		
Allen University	1870	Columbia, SC 29204
Benedict College	1870	Columbia, SC 29204
Claflin College	1869	Orangeburg, SC 29115
Clinton Jr. College	1894	Rock Hill, SC 29732
Denmark Technical College	1948	Denmark, SC 29042
Morris College	1908	Sumter, SC 29150
South Carolina State College	1896	Orangeburg, SC 29117
Voorhees College	1897	Denmark, SC 29042
TENNESSEE (7)		
Fisk University	1866	Nashville, TN 37203
Knoxville College	1875	Knoxville, TN 37921
Lane College	1882	Jackson, TN 38301
LeMoyne-Owen College	1862	Memphis, TN 38126
Meharry Medical College	1876	Nashville, TN 37208
Morristown College	1881	Morristown, TN 37814
Tennessee State University	1912	Nashville, TN 37203
TEXAS (9)		
Bishop College	1881	Dallas, TX 75241
Huston-Tillotson College	1876	Austin, TX 78702
Jarvis Christian College	1912	Hawkins, TX 75765
Paul Quinn College	1872	Waco, TX 76704
Prairie View A&M University	1876	Prairie View, TX 77445
Southwestern Christian College	1949	Terrell, TX 75160
Texas College	1894	Tyler, TX 75702
Texas Southern University	1947	Houston, TX 77004
Wiley College	1873	Marshall, TX 75670

VIRGIN ISLANDS (1)

University of the Virgin Islands	1962	St. Thomas, USVI 00801

VIRGINIA (6)

Hampton University	1868	Hampton, VA 23668
Norfolk State University	1935	Norfolk, VA 23504
Saint Paul's College	1888	Lawrenceville, VA 23868
The Virginia Seminary and College	1888	Lynchburg, VA 24501
Virginia State University	1882	Petersburg, VA 23803
Virginia Union University	1865	Richmond, VA 23220

WEST VIRGINIA (1)

West Virginia State College	1891	Institute, WV 25112

**OTHER EQUAL OPPORTUNITY EDUCATIONAL
COLLEGES AND UNIVERSITIES**

Atlanta Jr. College	1974	Atlanta, GA 30310
Chicago State University	1867	Chicago, IL 60628
Compton Community College	1927	Compton, CA 90221
Cuyahoga Community College	1971	Cleveland, OH 44115
Charles R. Drew University of Medicine and Science	1966	Los Angeles, CA 90059
Highland Park Community College	1918	Highland Park, MI 48203
Kennedy-King College	1935	Chicago, IL 60621
Lewis College of Business	1929	Detroit, MI 48235
Medgar Evers College	1969	Brooklyn, NY 11225
Roxbury Community College	1973	Boston, MA 02115
Sojourner-Douglass College	1972	Baltimore, MD 21205
Wayne County Community College	1969	Detroit, MI 48226

NOTES

1. Unless otherwise cited, all quotes in this chapter are from the correspondence of the Rockefeller Foundation with the Emergency Committee in Aid of Displaced Scholars at the Rockefeller Archives Center at Pocantico Hills, North Tarrytown, New York. Much of the data about the refugee scholars' placement by the Emergency Committee in Aid of Displaced Persons was located in the New York Public Library which houses documents and records of the Emergency Committee.
2. Robert Breitman and Alan M. Kraut, *American Refugee Policy and European Jewry, 1933–1945* (Bloomington: Indiana University Press, 1987), pp. 87–88.
3. Ibid.
4. Ibid., p. 74.
5. Ibid., p. 67.
6. Ibid., p. 53.

CHAPTER 3

Slave Codes to Black Codes

In order to set the scene for the world the refugee scholars found themselves in as newly arrived faculty members of the historically black colleges, it is necessary to present a picture of the racial situation in the country during the period at issue. Specifically, how did the general condition of race relations impinge on the educational institutions? Until the civil rights movement of the sixties succeeded in gaining the enactment of civil rights legislation, legal segregation remained in force in the South, where all but four of the black colleges were and are located.

After the emancipation of the slaves and a short period of limited gains by the freed African Americans, the slave codes were replaced by the legal caste system known as Black Codes. This system was enforced by the authorities and by terror. There were lynchings which went unpunished at least into the 1950s.

In what is generally considered to be the last acknowledged lynching in the South (but by no means the last act of racially motivated violence against African Americans), fifteen-year-old Emmet Till was beaten to death and dumped into the Tallahatchie River in 1954, ostensibly because he had whistled at a white woman. The two white men accused were found not guilty by the customary all-white jury.[1]

Only the hard and often bloody struggles of the civil rights movement activists, black and white, did away with this terror, in force so recently measured in terms of historical experience. Several anti-lynching bills had previously been introduced in Congress in the thirties and forties, all of them filibustered to death.

Black colleges existed in the usual two categories, public and private. The public ones were governed and funded by the state legislatures, which were white and whose commitment to vocational education for blacks was firmly entrenched. Their interests lay in maintaining a caste of agricultural, trades and service workers, menial and docile, considered vital to the interests of planters, business people, and industrialists. The private colleges were governed and funded by northern white philanthropists and church institutions, which allowed more liberal academic curricula, often maintained under difficult conditions. Moreover, teachers and clergy had to be educated, and the conflict between the academic and vocational needs reigned over the black educational establishment for many years, exemplified by Booker T. Washington and the Tuskegee/Hampton models for those colleges and, on the other, academic side, by W. E. B. DuBois, the brilliant advocate of racial equality in all things.

Aside from the widely accepted assumption of the racial inferiority of blacks, so convenient for their continued utilization as a cheap, docile work force, there was an interesting argument forwarded in favor of vocational education. Employment opportunities for African Americans were so limited, it would be cruel to educate people in the academic disciplines when they were barred from utilizing their education in their life's work. This was an argument sometimes advanced by northern white philanthropists who governed and funded the private black colleges. Black teachers were to be trained mainly to be agents inculcating their charges with the *ethic* of subservience and industry, piety, and good manners.

Funding differentials for black and white schools in the South for elementary and high schools in 1929–30 averaged $42.39 per capita per year for white pupils, $15.86 for blacks. Teacher salaries per month in 1928–29 averaged $118.01 for whites, $72.78 for blacks.[2] These figures relate to our study, since many of the students would have had their pre-college education in those circumstances. The private colleges fared somewhat better, although conditions varied considerably in different institutions from grade school through university.

One of the central problems in the black schools was the dearth of books. The Julius Rosenwald Fund, one of the chief philanthropic enterprises supporting black education in the South, provided special funding for the acquisition of books and the establishment of libraries. It must be remembered that libraries were also segregated and therefore separate libraries for blacks had to be maintained. It is very moving to learn of the ways poor blacks sacrificed savings, mortgaged crops and their meager holdings to raise matching funds for the Rosenwald Fund's schools and teacher training institutes in their communities.[3]

The school taxes black people paid were rarely allocated in sufficient amounts to benefit the schools for black children, so that their parents suffered a form of double taxation.[4] Myths that African Americans lacked commitment to education are destroyed by noting the enormous effort and sacrifice expended to educate the children of people not long removed from illiteracy and slavery.

As for federal funding, there was little of it until after World War II. The G. I. Bill provided educational opportunity for veterans of both races, to be sure, and for many families these comprised the first generation of college students.

Of the nineteen colleges which hosted refugee scholars, sixteen were private and three were state institutions. As noted, the private colleges were far likelier to offer an academic curriculum and thus were in a better position to accept and welcome European scholars with their humanist, cosmopolitan backgrounds.[5]

The contrast between the two groups of people discussed here is starkly illustrated by these data:

In 1930, 2.5 percent of blacks were occupied in professional service. This, of course, included all professions, not only academics.[6]

As of 1933, 12.5 percent of the Jewish population in Germany were academics.[7]

In other words, the percentage of blacks engaged in academic pursuits was minuscule compared to that of the German Jews who were about to enter black academia in the American South.

The educational level of a large proportion of the students cannot be inferred from the conditions and data described above. This encounter between central European intellectuals, so recently torn from their apparently safe and comfortable lives, and African Americans, so recently released from the most degrading conditions and still living an existence of constant guardedness against the ever-present sense of danger and the concomitant hard struggle to achieve a level of education as the sole hope for a more productive, freer existence, is at the heart of this work. Subsequent chapters will offer some of the stories, as told by participants in this coming together in a mutual endeavor.

How did the refugee aid organizations relate to black academia in the process of attempting to find positions for the refugee scholars? The enormous gulf between black and white America applied to the intellectual world in the North as it did to all spheres of American life. The German compound verb *totschweigen*, roughly translated as "killing by silence," applies here, as does James Baldwin's aptly phrased "studied ignorance." White ignorance of historically black colleges continues to this day. When I mention the existence of more than one hundred of these institutions, I am generally met with astonishment. It is noteworthy that the virtually universal condemnation of the racial policies of the Nazis engendered no apparent examination or connection between those and the cruel, pervasive racism at home.

The following letter did not bring a refugee scholar to Howard University. The earliest arrival I have been able to identify came in 1937. The letter was addressed to The Emergency Committee and signed by the Dean of the College of Liberal Arts at Howard University, Mr. E. P. Davis, dated August 17, 1934:

> Gentlemen:
>
> Would you kindly send me whatever printed or mimeographed statements you have for distribution touching the aid which you are rendering to colleges and universities in employing displaced German scholars?

A report on a trip to the South in 1939 to survey southern colleges and, incidentally, look into possible positions for the refugees, mentions Atlanta, Fisk, and Howard as black colleges visited in the twenty-three page report. This was to be a survey of natural science research activities in the southern colleges. It was conducted by Dean Edwin B. Fred of the University of Wisconsin for the Rockefeller Foundation. The South was by far the poorest section of the country, with a total population of more than 36 million people, 70 percent white, 30 percent colored, as the 1937 Census, quoted in the report, stated. Scientific research was deemed neglected in the South. A paragraph headed *Negro Institutions* reads:

> In this class belong Howard, Fisk and Atlanta University and the related colleges. All three are so different from the other universities in the South that they should be considered in a class by themselves.
>
> Atlanta and Fisk are in the South proper and are carrying on most important work for the colored people of the South. In research they are so new that it is unfair to judge their accomplishments, at least not in relation to the other institutions of higher learning. All three institutions—

Howard, Atlanta, and Fisk—have made a good beginning. A number of important researches are now underway.

A paragraph headed *Displaced German Scholars* reads:

Perhaps the research work would be greatly enriched by the addition of a good person fully qualified to carry on independent research. This author wishes to call attention to the possibilities that exist because of the large number of unusually capable men who have found it necessary to leave their European laboratories. There are some excellent research men belonging to this group. Perhaps some of these people could be wisely placed in southern institutions. This is an emergency measure to bring in strong research workers to initiate centers of research.

There was no mention that the above suggestion might relate to the black colleges.

A later memo in July 1941 tells of a trip to look at Tulane University in New Orleans in regard to setting up a "University Center" there for displaced foreign scholars, mentioning the possibility for "Paris in New Orleans," a center for French scholars in this hemisphere. This trip was organized by the Emergency Committee for Displaced Foreign Scholars. At that time, two refugee scholars had found positions at Xavier College, a black Catholic college in New Orleans. There is no mention of this fact in the memo to the Committee's Executive Committee to whom the memo is addressed.

In October 1933, the Emergency Committee voted funds for the support of displaced scholars to twenty universities for the 1933–34 academic year. Black colleges were not among these. Emergency Committee funds came from Jewish donors; foundation funds were separate. These funds were used to defray the first year's salary for the newcomers and matching contributions from the colleges were required. There appears to have been no comprehension on the part of the deciding bodies of men of the profound poverty of most of the black institutions. I have identified several instances of refugee scholars being unable to take the positions offered in black colleges for lack of matching funds.

An additional factor determining the exclusion of black colleges in the deliberations of the aid organizations was the matter of accreditation. The Southern Association of Colleges and Schools was founded in 1895 to set minimum standards for colleges.[8] In 1929, the Black College Association was established, limiting its members to those institutions approved by the Southern Association. Accreditation to those black colleges on the list approved by the Southern Association was granted in 1952, expanding the admission to full membership in 1957.[9] The refugees, having begun to arrive in 1933, needed help before that process was underway. A reference to the possibility of a job in a black college evoked the comment, "the kiss of death," on one occasion.

Thus, there were no organized efforts to target black schools as possibilities for opening up American academia for the refugee scholars. The letter to the institutions cited here did not go out until 1941, and there were a number of placements before then. There was, however, networking among the refugees, as well as other referral activity, some from the American Friends Service Committee, some simply by word of mouth. Most of these placements occurred in the forties, continued into the fifties and even as late as the sixties. Thus, it stands to reason that the increasing numbers of individuals and institutions in this process disseminated relevant information to interested parties, again both individual and institutional.

NOTES

1. Ralph Ginzburg, *One Hundred Years of Lynchings* (New York: Lancer Books, 1969), pp. 240–243.
2. Henry Allen Bullock, *A History of Negro Education in the South* (Cambridge: Harvard University Press, 1967), p. 180.
3. Ibid., pp. 140–141.
4. James D. Anderson, *The Education of Blacks in the South* (Chapel Hill: University of North Carolina, 1988), p. 156.
5. Wilma J. Roscoe, ed., *Accreditation of Historically and Predominantly Black Colleges and Universities*, National Association for Equal Opportunity in Higher Education (Lanham, Md.: University Press of America, 1989), pp. 52–53.
6. *The Negro Yearbook*, Tuskegee Institute, Tuskegee, Ala. (1932), pp. 260, 277.
7. Norbert Kampe, *Studenten und Judenfrage im Deutschen Kaiserreich* (Goettingen: Vandenhoeck & Ruprecht, 1988), p. 80.
8. Roscoe, *op. cit.*, pp. 3–5.
9. Ibid.

CHAPTER 4

Middle Passage—Statue Of Liberty

The relationship between African Americans and Jewish Americans has been marked by ambivalence. Two peoples sharing histories of persecution, oppression and violence against them, one still suffering from the legacy of slavery and racism, the other from prejudice and its repercussions, both with their memories of these sufferings and a sharp awareness of their histories deeply ingrained in them.

Like the majority of immigrants to America, Jews came to the new world to escape poverty, oppression, discrimination, and hopelessness. African Americans were cruelly torn away from their homeland and pressed into chattel slavery. These opposite poles in their collective consciousness are basic to their stories. One might metaphorically compare the image of the middle passage with the first view of the Statue of Liberty. For the Jews, after 1945, this image is shadowed by that of the cattle car and the gas chamber.

Our inquiry, however, concerns the years before knowledge of the extermination camps had come and there was still some hope for amelioration of the Jews' situation in Nazi-occupied Europe.

The racial situation in the United States has been described here to some extent, so I shall now turn to the attitudes toward the plight of the Jews under Nazi rule as expressed in African American publications before 1940. It will illustrate the atmosphere found by the refugee scholars in the black colleges, which became their workplaces—and sometimes their homes—in the thirties and after. The source for these observations is the remarkable 1941 M.A. dissertation by Lunabelle Wedlock in the Political Science Department at Howard University, headed at that time by Ralph Bunche.

The historical ambivalence mentioned above is based on the two-sided relationship between the two groups, always accompanied by the shared knowledge of their special status as minorities in the United States, different as their histories have been. There were the really important Jewish philanthropists, such as, in education matters, the Rosenwalds, as well as the numerous liberal and radical Jewish activists working for racial equality individually and in various organizations. One can attribute this Jewish activism to the prophetic tradition in Judaism (the Law), with its concern for justice and the basic tenet that human destiny, individual and collective, is a function of just action, with no reference to predestination or a hereafter characteristic of Christianity. Thence, Jewish emphasis on the here and now. The ever-present Jewish sense of the precariousness of life in the diaspora also played a role in the commitment to issues of economic and social justice.

The central difference between African Americans and Jews was and is class. Jews are perceived as a moneyed group and statistics did and still do bear out that levels of education and other indicators of living standards show great disparities between these two groups. From data for the 1950s, the following constitute some rough measurements:[1]

	Professional or Management	College Attendance	Mean Income (family of four)
Jews	46%	26%	$6,960
Blacks	7%	10%	$2,863

There are no figures available, so far as I could ascertain, for earlier years, as the Census did not use religious categories, which is how Jews are classified. Obviously, any difference between the fifties, the forties, and the thirties would show lower data for both groups in the earlier years, taking into consideration the Depression and the postwar G.I. Bill for veterans' education and benefits.

A major area of black-Jewish contact has been the landlord-tenant, shopkeeper-customer, employer-worker, and the housewife-domestic worker relationship, marked by antagonism much of the time, if not always. Among the most overtly scandalous manifestations of the black-Jewish worker-employer relationships was the infamous "Bronx Slave Market,"

... where the labor of Negro women was bought and sold in a fashion all too reminiscent of slavery in antebellum Dixie. The women doing the hiring were mainly Jewish residents of the Bronx. Rain or shine, cold or hot, you will find them there—Negro women, old and young—sometimes bedraggled, sometimes neatly dressed—but with the invariable paper bundle, waiting expectantly for Bronx housewives to buy their strength and energy for an hour, two hours, or even for a day at the munificent rate of 15, 20, 25 or, if luck be with them, 30 cents an hour.[2]

It is true that while one hears many stories of Jewish storekeepers, physicians and other agents of commerce or service being more flexible in their enforcement of segregation than Christians, it would be reckless to conclude that these stories reflected the rule. The basic fact was and remains that the class status of African Americans represents less prosperity, independence and fulfilment than that of Jews.

There were expressions of fear, well into the civil rights movement, on the part of Jews in the South that cooperation with the struggle for equality would inflame the bigots, such as the Ku Klux Klan, whose targets of hate were Jews and Catholics, as well as blacks. In Hattiesburg, Mississippi, a southern town of about 50,000 inhabitants with a small Jewish population, Rabbi Charles Martinband was active in the struggle against segregation in 1951–52 and was criticized by both his congregants and the community at large for his "open association with Negroes on an at-home social basis, his refusal to keep to himself his ideas about the evil of segregation, his very active participation in the Southern Regional Council, and the numerous speeches he made at nearby Negro colleges."

Paradoxically, the rabbi was given the key to the city when he left Hattiesburg in 1962. His successor, Rabbi Arthur Lelyveld, was beaten up in the struggle in 1964.[3]

In 1965 I met the unemployed Rabbi Ben-Ami in Washington, a German emigre with a heavy accent, in Washington in the Vietnam antiwar movement, and he told me that he had had to leave Hattiesburg because of his civil rights activities. Being without a pulpit, he agreed to participate in an ecumenical prayer service against the war, the only rabbi in Washington willing to speak out against the war at that time. Jewish timidity in these areas often had less to do with ideology than with fear of anti-Semitic reactions, although there's no reason to assume that Southern Jews were less racist on the whole than their Christian compatriots. (In connection with the Vietnam war, however, the hesitation was based on the fear that administration support for Israel might suffer if American Jews opposed the war openly.) This reasoning did not persist throughout the war, however.

These considerations are intended to illustrate some of the factors operating in "official" Jewish thinking and policy, as opposed to individuals, in those crucial historical events.

Without addressing the unresolved question—"Are Jews a race, a nation, a religious group or some other ethnic entity?"—the race issue is central to this historical period. The Nazi doctrine, as codified in the Nuremberg Laws, legislated the Jewish grandparent as the key determinant in identifying "Aryan" purity. In the American racial scheme, any black ancestor identifies a person as black, as testified to by such words as *octoroon*, which had legal status in Southern states where interracial marriage was outlawed as miscegenation, until declared unconstitutional by the Supreme Court in 1967.

Racial identity also was determined by visibility. There have been and continue to be Americans, white and black, who don't consider Jews to be white. Be that as it may, Jews do not have the degree of visibility of African Americans who are considered to be a race, although scientifically speaking, this is a false classification. There are people who "look Jewish," but people from various Mediterranean countries often share these characteristics as well. It is the visibility of African descent and the Jews' comparative invisibility which figure in their respective situations vis-à-vis the majority view.

While it is true that Jews participate in the privileges of white skin which dominate American life, regardless of other kinds of prejudice, and that this fact is something African Americans are aware of, it is also interesting to note that African Americans have traditionally considered Jews other than white. They are referred to as "the Jews," as opposed to the white man or, idiomatically, as "Goldberg," for example.

The above-mentioned master's dissertation by Lunabelle Wedlock, written in 1941 under the supervision of Ralph Bunche, is entitled "The Reaction of Negro Publications and Organizations to German Anti-Semitism." This is a brilliant study which reveals much valuable material concerning the thinking of black leaders and intellectuals in the face of Nazi racist practice. The thesis abounds in quotes from African Americans comparing German and American race theory and practice:

The fascist governments of the world view American indignation over racial oppression with wonder and bewilderment. They cannot understand why America should be so concerned with racial persecution in Europe and yet defend it with such vigor within its own borders. . . .

It is a long story—perhaps no good will come from the telling. But this much is certain: the voice of America would carry far greater authority when it speaks against racial oppression in Europe if it could be heard against racial oppression at home.[4]

Kelly Miller, an outstanding professor of sociology at Howard University, wrote much on the evils of American and Nazi racism, pointing out on one occasion "the high visibility of the Negro in contrast with the low visibility of the Jew in Germany," adding that "Hitler wants the Jew to get out of Germany entirely," a remarkably prescient observation, quoted in *The Washington Tribune* on June 23, 1933! A curious comment in that same article quotes Kelly Miller: "Georgia fears the Negro will lower the level of Anglo-Saxon civilization. Hitler fears the Jews will raise it too high."[5]

Nazi race theories were utilized to enact legislation intended to assure forever the racial purity of "Aryan" Germans, which policy, coincidentally, added considerably to the coffers of the Nazi plunderers. American racial practice was based on the need to maintain an "inferior" people as a subjugated class of workers.

While the Black Codes and extralegal methods which enforced segregation and exclusion in the southern states violated the spirit of the Fourteenth and Fifteenth Amendments to the Constitution, there was no such constitution troubling the Nazis. An editorial in the February 22, 1936, issue of the *Afro-American* states that:

Our Constitution keeps the South from passing many of the laws Hitler has invoked against the Jews, but by indirection, by force and terrorism, the south and Nazi Germany are mental brothers.[6]

On the disenfranchisement of both groups, we read in the same paper of May 3, 1936:

Berlin recently advised Jewish citizens that they would be arrested and prosecuted if they went to the polls and voted in the coming national elections. The difference between Germany and Dixie is that Nazis disenfranchised Jews by national law and the South keeps us from the polls by state law and by intimidation.[7]

In *The Crisis* of February 1939, the writer points out that,

... there is, of course, an important difference, as thoughtful Jews them-selves have explained. Negroes in this country still have—in most sec-tions—the right to protest and work to improve their lot. In Germany the Jews have no such privilege. There is no hope.[8]

This last point—no hope—strikes an ominous note when looked at retrospectively at a time when few of the policymakers confronted this probability in 1939.

The fact that the economic situation of Jews was and is far better than that of African Americans has, perhaps inevitably, encouraged the stereotypes of the single-minded, money-grabbing Jew to be adopted by some African Americans, sometimes by copying the majority image of this notorious type. But the other perspective was represented more frequently: awareness of the disparity between the two groups, but not exploiting this fact so as to fall into the trap of racial prejudice, so terribly injurious to all, and all too often exploited by those whose interests appear to lie in divisions among groups working to change the status quo.

Much was written in the black press comparing the situation of African Americans to that affecting Jews in Germany under Nazi rule. *The Philadelphia Tribune* on December 29, 1938, featured an article titled "Hitler Learns Jim Crow Art from America" and states:

Bachrach Brothers, one of the leading department stores in Magdeburg, Germany, was closed, last week, by police who found six Jewish employ-ees married to white German girls.

The cops said the populace was so excited that law and order were menaced.

All over Germany one excuse or another is used in order to close up Jewish stores and compel them to sell out to Germans.

We are accustomed to such tricks in the South wherever white neighbors covet the stores or the farms of colored persons. Down South we don't say "the populace was excited." Our common expression is that "feeling runs high."[9]

An article begins as follows:

The persecution of the Jews in Germany by the Nazi Government is deplorable, stupid and outrageous.
The persecution of colored Americans by Americans is cruel, relentless and spirit breaking.[10]

A survey of the 1938 volume of *Das Schwarze Korps*, the weekly SS newspaper, shows the contempt the Nazis held for American tears over the treatment of German Jews, considering American treatment of African Americans. Aside from noting they compared American practices of segregation to their own and mocked American democracy and humanitarianism as hypocritical, it is important to know that African Americans were monitoring Nazi publications and publicizing these findings in its press.

From the *Philadelphia Tribune* on April 6, 1933, we find:

The lynchings of Negroes, disenfranchisement and economic oppression have caused only a few Americans to shed any tears over the plight of Negroes. It is easy for America to condemn Hitler for his atrocities against the Jew, but American atrocities against colored citizens remain unchallenged.[11]

On a different note, the *Afro-American* on August 24, 1935, comments:

We rejoice that our newspapers condemn German Nazi atrocities. It's a good sign that they may yet discover the Nazism which is outside their own doors.

An editorial in the *Afro-American* on April 9, 1938, entitled "Heil Hitler!" says:

. . . isn't it safer for Uncle Sam in the long run? Isn't it cheaper? Isn't it easier on his blood pressure for him to deal justly with the oppressed people at home than to shed tears in public, tear his hair and beat his breasts over the way Hitler is oppressing the people of Germany and Austria? . . . We detest him for the way in which he is crushing the Jews . . . But we can't forget there is a man right here who has his heel on our neck.[12]

A September 1938 editorial in the *Crisis* entitled "Refugees and Citizens" states:

> Let those whose hearts bleed so for the men and women across the sea turn their glances within their borders. They will see Hitlerism on every side directed against citizens who happen not to be white.[13]

With respect to higher education, there is cited from the *Afro-American* on July 15, 1933, an editorial, "Appeal for Negroes and Appeal for Jews":

> Each of the above named universities is in the South. Each protesting against the atrocities in Germany against the Jews commit daily the same atrocities against Negroes.
> Each of them is lily-white despite the fact that it is supported in whole or in part by public tax funds.
> Each virtually is a party to the crime by means of which tax funds due Negro children are stolen and spent only on white education.[14]

On labor unions, the *Philadelphia Tribune* on July 5, 1934, in an editorial titled "Germany vs. America," says " . . . Until labor unions let down the racial bars, labor leaders should keep quiet concerning human rights."[15]

There are many more examples of German mockery and African American outcry at the double standard applied to Jewish oppression in Nazi Germany and black oppression in the United States. Once again, Kelly Miller is cited in the *Norfolk Journal and Guide* on December 17, 1938, in an article titled "Americans Set Pace, Nazis Answer," as follows:

> But granting counter charges of Hitler and his cohorts, how would that justify their barbarities against the Jews which shock the conscience of the world . . . Citing cruelties and outrages against Negroes in Georgia is a poor justification for atrocities against Jews in Germany.[16]

There are frequent comparisons of the Nazis to the Ku Klux Klan to be found in the African American press of the period. One poignant example is an editorial in the *Afro-American* on January 16, 1937, called "The German Hate":

Germany is persecuting Jews, Catholics and Negroes. Hitler is a European Ku Kluxer—Hitler's Ku Kluxism is storing up for Germany mountains of hate that will deluge the Teutons for centuries.[17]

It is sobering as well as provocative to read this view of the Third Reich in 1937 by African Americans and to contemplate the significance for us today.

An article in the *Das Schwarze Korps* on November 24, 1938, is accompanied by a vicious cartoon showing the stereotypical Jew, whose shirt says "USA" above the Star of David, protesting in the name of humanity the barbaric methods of Germany. Behind him are two equally objectionable stereotypical figures of two African American men, one being lynched with a rope around his neck, one being electrocuted. The word "barbarism" is derided in the article as being constantly applied to Nazi practice and citing British colonialists' and missionaries' "blessings" as applied to "savages" in their overseas possessions.

This same article warns the democracies that their professed compassion for German Jews is not manifest in their practices and policies governing the welcoming of victims, i.e., the Jews. Accurately, the restrictions are cited to prove that these alleged democrats are not about to welcome thousands of persecuted Jews into their midst. Ominously, we are told that Germany has no land to spare for Jews who must be totally removed from German soil, implying that only the opening of doors by the democracies will save the Jews from their destruction, which was dictated by Nazi ideology. They could not have been clearer.

It is reasonable to assume that the refugee scholars' colleagues and students were not unfamiliar with the publications cited and the opinions expressed therein on Nazi policies toward German Jews. It is also reasonable to assume that these opinions and discussions of the subject were topics among faculty and maybe students in the black colleges. What is not clear is the extent to which these observations were shared with the refugee scholars.

I searched the literature to find data on the ratio of black to white faculty in the colleges at issue in this work. I was unable to find such information. For what it's worth, I can cite one finding, from the "Survey of Negro Colleges and Universities," published in 1929 by the Department of the Interior, Bureau of Education, covering data from 1927. It reports that the proportion of white teachers was decreasing in the independent and Northern denominational colleges. No data were provided. It continues by saying that the public and black denominational colleges continued to be staffed with black faculty only. There is no reference to the independent black colleges, but we know that faculty there was both black and white. It must also be remembered that it took decades to train black teachers to achieve faculty status; they were not likely able to afford a Northern college, assuming they were admitted, and few historically black colleges offered graduate courses until the 1950s.

Of the fifty-one scholars in this study, twenty-one began their tenure at black colleges before 1945. The significance of that date lies in the fact that it was only after the defeat of the Germans that the full extent of the extermination of the Jews and other people became general knowledge. The awful discovery changed the perceptions of Nazi policy and practice totally. While people had realized that European Jewry under Nazi rule had undergone great suffering, been segregated, deported, impoverished, and that many people had been murdered, the films, photos and reports of the Nazi crimes presented a new dimension of human destruction in the twentieth century with the technological methods developed by a government expressly for that purpose. The word "genocide" was coined and the United Nations adopted legal conventions which made genocide subject to international law, even if the act was committed by a sovereign state in its own territory.

Numerous instances in history tell us of the destruction of religious, racial, or ethnic groups by governmental agencies. Specific to our study, one might point out that since the new word's coinage, the term has frequently been used to characterize the shipping of Africans to the Americas, which resulted in enormous numbers of casualties. The fact that it was coined in response to the Nazi crimes tells us of a *caesura* in history, linguistic, conceptual, and juridical. The changed human consciousness since the end of World War II encompasses a range of awareness of the destructiveness of technological developments, including the nuclear capability known popularly as "The Bomb." The Bomb and genocide have thus become embedded in our minds, conscious and subconscious. If we add to these fears the specters of "ecocide," another new word, the knowledge leading to the prevention of these man-made catastrophes as part of the historian's learning suggests sobering and daunting tasks for this discipline.

Protective Troops (Blackshirts SS) of the National Socialist Party, Organ of the Reich leadership.

The Black Corps
The Last Scream

Der letzte Schrei

„...und so protestieren wir im Namen der Menschlichkeit gegen die barbarischen Methoden Deutschlands!"

" . . . and so we protest, in the name of humanity against the barbaric methods of Germany!"

Das Schwarze Korps
The Black Corps   November 17, 1938

The Jews' Paradise

Das Judenparadies

Zeichnung: I

Mensch, Sam, wenn das so weiter geht, dann heißt es bald nicht mei
„Vereinigten —", sondern die „Verunreinigten Staaten von Amei

Man, Sam, if this goes on, soon it won't be called "United"—but the
"Soiled States of America." (Impossible to copy similarity of words in
English)

November 1938   Number 46 page 7

'THE BLACK CORPS'
In the New York Subway

First Panel
—You see, Mr. Cohn, we Americans are a free people. And Roosevelt speaks from the soul, when he says: We know neither difference in religion nor of race!

Second panel
The best proof of the rejection of race theory by the American people is that our best track star, our world champion boxer, comes from the ranks of the . . .

Fifth panel
These Niggers are always getting fresher! This impudent one thinks he can sit down in the compartment for whites! Oh well. Where was I? Oh yes, we Americans are against racism, well. . . . (etc.)

NOTES

1. Andrew M. Greeley, *Ethnicity in the United States: A Preliminary Reconnaissance* (New York: John Wiley & Sons, 1974), p. 78.
2. Robert S. Weisbord and Arthur Stein, *Bittersweet Encounter: The Afro-American and the American Jew* (Westport, Conn.: Negro Universities Press, 1970), p. 47.
3. Ibid., pp. 137–138.
4. Lunabelle Wedlock, *Reaction of Negro Publications and Organizations to German Anti-Semitism* (Washington, D.C.: Howard University Press, 1941), p. 103.
5. Ibid., p. 113.
6. Ibid., p. 111.
7. Ibid., p. 112.
8. Ibid., p. 93.
9. Ibid.
10. Ibid., p. 95.
11. Ibid., p. 96.
12. Ibid., p. 97.
13. Ibid., p. 98.
14. Ibid.
15. Ibid., p. 104.
16. Ibid.

CHAPTER 5

" . . . Now Suddenly I Was on the Other Side, I Belonged Not to the Oppressed but to the Oppressor."

I have now described the conditions the refugee scholars and their families found upon arrival in the United States and, specifically, in the historically black colleges where they were to teach and, in some instances, to live. It was a doubly alien world—black segregated America, dependent and yet so removed from white America. It must be kept in mind that of necessity black America was familiar with the white world, having worked and lived by its rules and in its homes and institutions ever since arriving on these shores. Conversely, whites were and continue to be largely ignorant of the culture and living conditions of African Americans. As newly arrived refugees from a very different world, they were doubly marginal to both worlds and had to learn them both and adjust, as the word went, to both. How this process worked for them and the students and colleagues they were to function with, will be addressed in this part of the work.

Among fifty-some individuals in twenty-some historically black colleges, there are thirty of whom I know next to nothing beyond the fact that they had emigrated as refugees from Germany or Austria after 1933 or 1938 respectively, and that they had taught certain subjects for a certain period of time in certain of these colleges. There are two primary reasons for this paucity of information: the time passed since this historical episode occurred, and the fact that most of these normally financially strapped institutions lack the archival resources, both material and human, to provide the necessary documents so many years later. Had it been possible for me to visit each of these campuses for personal investigation, it might have produced more material. Unfortunately this was not possible. Thus, I know nothing of these scholars' thoughts and feelings about their new environment and their interaction with it. But even if these experiences and insights are lost to us, one can hope that the positive influences on both parties live on in those who were touched in this encounter.

Living conditions varied greatly in the urban colleges from those removed from towns and cities. At the urban ones, the refugee scholars found housing in the surrounding areas. Some campuses, while adjacent to a town, had no contact with the totally segregated life there. At Talladega, Alabama, the college is adjacent to the town of Talladega, but separate from it. Thus, the faculty lived on campus, where there were also schools from pre-school through high school for all faculty children, black and white. There was a clinic, a movie schedule, and other social amenities available to the college population, and the white faculty was known not to patronize "white only" establishments. Needless to say, the local townspeople viewed them with hostility. Mr. Jim McWilliams was a student at Talladega from 1950 to 1954 and knew a number of refugee professors who were teaching there at the time. Here are some observations he made in an interview:

> Now keep in mind that this is a school in which the complete outside surroundings were hostile. So, everybody had to live together in a way that is different than a university now. And that's why I mentioned that classrooms and social life were hard to distinguish. And getting together on Sunday was an important aspect of that because we always had fantastic choral music and that music was more likely to be classical music of Beethoven and Bach as well as spirituals.
>
> If somebody wanted to go to the movies, there was no such thing. There was a movie theater in Talladega. We could not go. There were no segregated seats. And that would have been the period of segregated water fountains and toilets and the whole thing. So, we had our own movie on the campus, we had our own dances, we had our own everything. It was a totally self-contained community. We had our dentist and a doctor.
>
> So far as I know, the refugees never went to a segregated facility. In order to get any social relief, I think that the faculty members would leave the area, go to New York. But they were probably regarded in a very unpleasant fashion by the townspeople of Talladega, that they were so closely integrated.

Similar conditions prevailed at Hampton, Virginia; Lincoln, Pennsylvania; West Virginia State; and Tougaloo, Mississippi. Lincoln, some miles from Oxford, the nearest town, included a village called Lincoln which maintained two elementary schools, a wooden one for blacks, a brick one for whites.

Professor Walter Fales taught philosophy at Lincoln University in Pennsylvania from 1946 until his death in 1953. His widow, Ruth Fales, continues to live next to the campus and finds her activities and her friends on that campus to this day. I have visited and interviewed her. She organized a dinner for me with a number of retired faculty friends who shared their recollections of Professor Fales's times with me. Mrs. Fales was a kindergarten teacher, and here is some of what she told me:

> I became a member of London Grove (Friends) Meeting, and it was at London Grove where I was asked to start a kindergarten after a Meeting member had a sort of part-time kindergarten there, but had passed away. And we then started a kindergarten which was open not only to the children of the Meeting, but to the children in the whole area. At that time, the public schools did not have kindergarten. The churches did, but there was no kindergarten in the area where black children were also welcome. And we made a point of making sure. I went to some of the black churches and talked there. They asked me to come and explain. And so, our kindergarten started with children of the Meeting and children from the surrounding area. There were scholarships available. And the kindergarten is still in full bloom. And I'm there quite often. I retired after 23 years.

I asked Mrs. Fales if they and other white faculty members availed themselves of the segregated facilities in the area, for interestingly, while it was Pennsylvania, Lincoln lies in the south of the state very near the Maryland line and practiced the social habits of the segregated South. Here is her reply:

> Absolutely not. As a matter of fact, we—I took my children to the cinema we used to have in Oxford (the nearby town) to find out that blacks were only supposed to be in a particular place. I took my daughter and her black friend together to see a children's picture and sat right in the middle of the movie theater.
> There was a member of the Friends' Meeting, believe it or not, who had a swimming pool. We asked to go there and swim with our friends, and they wouldn't. They said it was private and they wouldn't permit. We did not go swimming anywhere unless—I would go into one of the others, farther away, a public one, and have one of the (black) faculty members there, come right behind me. There is no room—it was all filled

up then. And no, I was going after him, and they let me in, and then I said, "hey, I thought it was full." So, we did all sorts of things like that.

I would like to add here that her father, her mother, and her sister went to Holland to escape from Nazi Germany. Her sister married a Dutchman, and when the Nazis came to get them, he had an opportunity to get away. He refused, and the four of them were sent to Sobibor where they died.

The discussion with the friends at the dinner brought out some significant observations, some of which I shall quote, as follows:

There was very little contact between Lincoln University campus and Oxford, which is three miles away. We were pretty well self-contained. We had our own movie theater. The Red Cross came to a private pool for two weeks in the summer, and that's where our children learned to swim. We had our own recreation. We had a doctor and an infirmary and our own nursery school. In fact, it went up through the second grade, and then, when the schools were consolidated in Oxford, then all of the grades went there.

In Lincoln (the village), there was a brick school for the white children and a frame building across the street where the black children went. Dr. Horace Mann Bond (the distinguished President of Lincoln) brought a law suit. They decided to let the black faculty children go to the white school in the village. And the black children who lived in the village remained at the black school. Class replaced race, in that instance.

The Ku Klux Klan was three miles down the road. In the forties, I remember when we resisted—if I may use the word—at the movie theater in Oxford, and Dr. Bond led that. They chased us back. As a matter of fact, they had guns with them, and they chased us back to the campus. Oh, the Klan was very popular down here. In 1954, I was married, and my husband and I lived in a large apartment building just across the street and one night we saw a cross right out front.

Then later, we moved into a building on the campus, and next to us lived a white family. The oldest daughter was dating a black fellow who was a student. They have since married and have children. But I remember one night we heard noise, and we went outside and somebody had left a cross in their yard, and we were all trying to put the fire out. It was in the 50s, the late 50s.

My husband and I used to walk our dog every night, and one night we were walking our dog, down the campus walk, and later I found out that somebody had ridden behind the President's house and had thrown something in Dr. Bond's back window. I don't remember whether it was a bomb or what. But as my husband and I were walking, we were just about in front of the guest house here on the sidewalk, a car with a bunch of kids, and they were white kids, slowed up and threw something out of the window, as they pulled past us. And it turned out to be a cherry bomb that just missed my foot. And from that night, we never walked the campus walk with our dog, we always walked on the lawn from then on.

This has been a compendium of a number of different peoples' comments from that evening. So it was circumstances such as those described that are of particular significance in the family life of the refugee scholars. A 1957 letter from Professor Peter Kahn, head of the art department of Hampton, explained his resignation to President Moron:

Bringing up children in the South is more difficult than we had envisaged some years ago, when we first came to the South. Both my wife and I had hoped fervently that we could in our small way help to make an integrated society possible. We have waited impatiently for some changes that have not taken place, neither outside, nor right here on campus.

Kahn went to teach at Cornell. It must be added that he found his administrative duties at Hampton to preclude his pursuit of the research he wanted to do.

Erika Thimey taught dance at Howard University from 1944 to 1955. She is not Jewish, and came to the United States originally in 1931, having worked with a dancer in Berlin who married an American and brought her to the United States on a visitor's visa. Thimey had this visa renewed periodically, and finally decided to go back to Berlin. Here's what she told me about one such trip:

When I found how Germany had changed—I think I had to go back every two years at least—and—well, eventually things changed too much. I was not a politically interested person, so it really had to be obvious when I noticed something. For example, it was in 1936 that I gave a program in Berlin, and then I realized how the situation had changed. In order to get the permission to perform, I had to list the whole program, all the music, the composers, and so on, the names of the different numbers, oh yes, something going on. And I thought, boy, I have—I'm much freer in America than in Germany. You never know. But I mean I just decided to stay in America.

After some years in Chicago and in Boston, performing with several groups, as well as teaching, Thimey came to Howard University in 1944. Here are her reminiscences:

I started out at Howard University in 1944. I was invited to help with the performance in the spring—I think it had to do with graduation—and I was very impressed with how nice the students were to me. And they had had very little to do with modern dance, but they took to it very lovely.

I want to add here that Thimey had studied with Mary Wigman in Berlin, whom I would call the German Martha Graham, in terms of the role she played in the development of modern dance in Germany.

And then I was invited to become a regular teacher on a part-time basis. I was at Howard about eleven years, and during that time, I noticed a great change. In the beginning, the students were very timid and shy and they only did things that I demonstrated to them and when it came to creative work, they held back very much. Then gradually I noticed, I couldn't quite figure out why, but they became much more aggressive, a little bit in a positive way and they became interested in creative work, that they were doing things themselves. And when jazz music was coming on the horizon—I don't know whether it was the time, but in any case, they became different people, much more the way I know black people now.

We did not have any live piano in the classroom. In my own studio, I did. Always, every class had live accompaniment. But there I had to use a drum or to use records. And I was always interested to know what was going on, what the new things were that were offered. So, when I came with a record that was jazz music, I could just see how just instinctively everybody was brightening up. Before it was probably classical music or some modern music, so-called modern music. But that was always concert music, Debussy or Ravel or Stravinsky. And we cooperated very much with the music department. So, of course, sometimes they made suggestions and that was wonderful. The music department was excellent, and I like to experiment myself, so whatever I could, I like to do.

When the teacher from the art department brought over some sculpture pieces or some larger paintings, then my dancers had to look at that and then they had to dance with it. Sometimes with painted pieces, they were not allowed to touch, but with the sculptures they were allowed to. And so, sometimes I smile when I see what they are doing now with experimental modern movements, the "avant garde." Well, over at Howard University, we certainly experimented around. And, of course, I had my background from Mary Wigman, who always encouraged experimentation very much. She was my teacher. I mean, obviously we had to learn to improve our technique too, but she wanted to develop artists I guess, that was the main thing, and not to develop little followers.

What was wonderful for me, at that time the whole idea of—when you are a white person, to surround yourself with black people, either you

were a radical or you were crazy. When we started out, that was sort of
the double feeling I felt. And I was really quite amazed that I was not
crazy and that I was not radical, but this was a wonderful experience.
And then when I told other people about what happened, they were
surprised. That was, of course, before—what do you call that thing? Yes,
the civil rights movement. Yes. So, I feel very privileged that I had that
opportunity to understand that a little bit more personally.

When I was a student at Mary Wigman's, we had many people from
foreign countries and there were also a few black people. And they did
not come from America, they came from Africa, from North Africa. And
I was amazed how wonderful they were and we really felt that was a
privilege that we had such interesting company, I mean students and
colleagues. And when I came to America and people told me that black
people are nothing, I was a little bit surprised. And when I went traveling
by train or with a bus, the black people always had to sit in a different
part than the white people, and that was the separation. Well, it was
interesting for me. I tried to understand why and what, and so on. So,
when I had the opportunity to find really out and get in touch with black
people, I grabbed at the opportunity and I sure made many good friends.
I still have, from time to time, some colleagues and some former students,
with whom I'm in touch.

I was invited to bring the Howard group, the dance group, over to New
York for several performances there. Ivan Nicolai was the director of the
dance department of Henry Street Playhouse at that time, and he was
very much interested in inviting different groups. And he must have heard
of me through Hanya Holm, who had been my former teacher when she
was still in Germany, before she opened up her own studio in New York.
She started out with the Mary Wigman studio in New York. In any case,
we performed together with different colleges and the Howard group was
one. And it was amazing how people reacted. My group was definitely
not the worst one. It was more or less the best one. And we were invited
several times again, and we were doing quite a bit of traveling, which
was very complicated at that time.

I remember when we went to Hampton, that was organized through
someone with a chartered bus. But when we stopped and wanted to go
to a restroom, oh, that was so complicated, because I had to go quite
somewhere else from the others. And I never realized this until you're
exposed to something like that, how complicated life is. And then how
at the end of my work at Howard, I remember that we were doing a
dance—I think it was in Alexandria, Virginia, and I went together with
one of my students into a hotel and I thought, oh, I hope they will not
be insulting to that girl. So, I went to the desk first and asked and there
was no problem whatsoever. So, then I realized that really segregation
was going to end.

But what was interesting for me was all the opportunities I had for my
development and then I realized that the students caught on and that this

was not only for me personally, but that this was exciting for the students too. Thank heaven, because after all, I was supposed to be a teacher. At the Dance Club at Howard, where the students were signed up for at least one semester, they came and it didn't make any difference what I did with them. They would not say that we did not improve our technique, or we were not interested in this. I never heard anything like that. So, they were always fascinated. And when the time was up that I should stop this, they said, "oh, the time went much too fast." So, I had opportunities of trying things out that I could not do in my own studio. It enriched me very much. I mean from an artistic viewpoint. I mean, already to have the opportunity to collaborate with artists—the art department. If I wanted to do that in my own studio, I would have to go to an artist, and I was not befriended with artists that way. And the music department, where the choir was so terrific.

And then, of course, I was interested to learn more about the history of the black people and then I found out about the underground railroad and Harriet Tubman. And I thought, well, I'm sure that they're even more interested, so I made a pageant more or less based on her biography. And then the music department collaborated and we did that at the Rankin Chapel, that tiny little chapel. And they rebuilt the inside there completely. They made a scaffold in the back where originally the elders would have been, but there was the choir standing. And in front of it, they made the platform large enough that a dance group could dance on it. And I don't know whether there was any place left for the audience. That was really a large sort of thing.

We had many performances going on and one time the director of the symphony asked me if I could do the same music that Disney used for *Fantasia*, "The Sorcerer's Apprentice," that's it. And I had done the choreography, and I had been playing around with ideas, so that was just accidental that they asked me whether I could do that for the symphony there. And, well, one thing led to the other and I did not do "The Sorcerer's Apprentice" for the symphony, I did that with my own company without the symphony at a different place. But I kept the contact and was doing a completely different program with the Howard University group. When I suggested that I had more people at Howard than in my own company and that to perform that there would be more impressive to have a larger company, they said, well, why not. And so then it was much later that I found out that there had been some complications when black people were invited at Constitution Hall. It was really very funny.

(I remind the reader of the episode involving Marian Anderson's denial of permission to perform at Constitution Hall and Mrs. Roosevelt's intervention and resignation from the Daughters of the American Revolution, the owners of the Hall, so that she sang at the

Lincoln Memorial to an audience of thousands, with Mrs. Roosevelt present on stage. This became a famous case in the history of the struggle to end segregation in Washington, D.C.).

Back to Ms. Thimey:

I remember we did a series of dances, not only one dance. And one of them was "The Lightening Polka" of Johann Strauss. There were no problems whatsoever. In the beginning, I was very much interested in dance performances for child audiences. And my company (from my studio) had a traveling company and we performed in different cities, and when there were reviews, we always got very nice reviews.

We were touring all the schools in the District of Columbia. But I found out very soon that the population in the District was 80 percent black. And if there was only a white company that they would not relate to that so easily. So, I thought it would be much wiser if at least it would be mixed. So, I always looked, made sure that I had a mixed company. But now where do you get good dancers who are black? Of course, Howard University was my contact there, and so that was a very good help for me. And oh, it was so funny when we performed in some schools and somebody would say, "oh, my mother was a student of yours at Howard." At Howard University, when I wanted to have a mixed group, then I was told that there was a women's department and a men's department. And I said, well, the dancing is mixed that's exactly like drama, and he (not identified) said, "yes, yes, we will see what we can do." And then we did get some male dancers.

And I remember they were very shy in the beginning too and it took some time before they really loosened up and were comfortable. So, I was always wondering, is that my technique, and so I encouraged them very much to do what they wanted to do, so I just gave them a certain time limitation. I said you have eight minutes or 20 measures. And eventually that helped also. Black people were freer. And also, I think it helped that they felt they were successful. I mean a black person had to stand so much negativism. And you know, in a way that was interesting for me, too. An artist, when you start out, you are not successful right away, you can't be. But sometimes they say, oh, you're talented, you are promising. And with a black person, to get confidence, self-confidence, well, that took some time too.

With the administration I had no contact whatsoever in the beginning. I got a check, I don't know whether it was every month or something like that and that was it. But then, towards the end, I was offered a job in Silver Spring, teaching children's classes, and that was in conflict with my schedule at Howard. And I was not sure what I could do about that. So, I asked whether it was possible to have time off for a vacation, so that I could find out what that was really all about there. And they told me, no, that was impossible. He said, "but you are part-time." So, that

was the only thing that I was not very happy about. And then I also
asked whether there was a chance of getting a change in the salary.
Because I had heard that other people had gotten a raise and so on. And
he said, "but you are part-time." And then I mean my life became a little
bit complicated. I had to start thinking in a financial way too. Because I
mean I wanted to get my company going. And so, that was really finally
the reason that I thought that I had to make a decision. I had been there
eleven years and had never had a raise.

Ernst Borinski was the only refugee scholar to teach at Tougaloo,
where he stayed for thirty-six years and was buried in the small cemetery on the campus. Single, he occupied some rooms in a dormitory for
many years; later, the college provided him with a house near the campus. Borinski maintained active and focused relations with a number of
white individuals and institutions in Jackson, a few miles away. He
cultivated these relationships also to promote his agenda of furthering
racial amity and ending segregation and the evils this entailed. Borinski
was a major figure in the history of the college, the civil rights struggle
in the area and the lives of many of his students and associates. There
is much to tell about this extraordinary man, so he'll have a section all
to himself in another chapter.

As for North Carolina Central in Durham, I interviewed both Professor Ernst Moritz Manasse and his son, Dr. Gabriel Manasse. Professor Manasse taught German, Latin, and philosophy at NCC from 1939
to 1973 and continues to live in Durham. He had received his Ph.D. in
Heidelberg in November 1933, which foreclosed his chance of teaching
in Germany. Here are some of his observations made in our interview:

When I came to this country, I had no contact with any black person at
all. I had a friend who was offered a position at NCC, that was Ernest
Abrahamson, who taught at Howard. I was then offered this position. I
was entirely unprepared when I came here. Of course, I didn't know about
American colleges anyhow. I mean, not as black colleges, but about
American colleges and learned how the situation is when I was here. It
was, in a way, very uncomfortable for me. Some people thought, well, if
you take the position here at the black college, you are no better than
the blacks, that I'm not good enough to teach at a white college. I mean,
none directly said so, but I felt it in their attitude.

For me it was a great difficulty that I could not invite my colleagues
and my students to the house. A colleague of mine brought me home in
a car—we had no car for the first 14 years—and I asked him in for a

cup of coffee. I was called to come to the rental office; the neighbors had complained that I had a Negro visitor who was not working in my house. And six weeks later the same thing happened again, and I was called again and told the neighbors won't stand for this and, if it happens again, he would shoot. Not at me, but at my colleague.

Well, I came from a situation of forceful segregation where we were the victims and now suddenly I was on the other side; I belonged not to the oppressed but to the oppressor. And that was certainly very, very uncomfortable for me. And I think that my colleagues waited for a while and wanted to see how things developed. Later, I got the confidence of most of them and I think perhaps more than some of the other white people who also were teaching in later years. I was the first full-time white teacher.

During the war, it happened here in Durham that a black soldier on furlough took a bus and the driver told him to go back. He had done nothing threatening but talked to the driver who pulled out a revolver and shot him, killed him. Then this man who had shot him was tried and acquitted.

I was referred to a Jewish family which helped me find a room, sent some food, pens, things like that. My wife and little son had not yet arrived from Brazil. My mother was a really religious person and my father was the president of the Jewish congregation in the little town of Dramburg, Pomerania, now Poland. And both my wife and I had had Christmas trees. But this was here resented by the Jewish people. My wife took our children to the Jewish Sunday School for two years, I think, which the children hated. And then we didn't insist that they keep going. And the relations became more and more loose. We used to say, "we're isolated because they are prejudiced against us. We are Germans—in the Second World War—we're Jews, we have Negroes at our house, and we have no money."

In the sixties we were required to, every department was asked to offer some course which had to do with the black problem. And I knew very little at that time about black philosophers. And I then suggested a course about the black power argument, and we will subtitle the course in applied logic. At first I gave it as an informal, noncredit course. We met once a week in the evening. And the maximum number of students admitted to classes at that time was 40, and 40 students had pre-registered for it. And we had chosen four books, one of Martin Luther King's—I forgot the title—one was Fanon's *Wretched of the Earth*, *The Autobiography of Malcolm X*, and a black power book by Stokeley Carmichael.

And I had arranged the course so that I would give an introduction. We discussed reading assignments, and there was tension, of course, as there had never been before, not so much between the students and myself, but between the more militant and the less militant students, which led to a situation that one day half of the students left because of something that not I, but some student had said. That was around 1967. And after this had gone on for a month or so, the students came to me and said that I'm talking too much in this discussion. And then I said "alright, instead of my giving the introduction, let some students give it, copy and distribute it, and that's what we'll be doing here."

But then it happened that the thing became boring, became dead. I mean, at first I always got myself into the class with some tension, but then there was no more tension and all the tension had gone away, but out of this also all the interest in it. And at the end of the semester, instead of giving a final examination, I said they should criticize the course, and this was rewarding. Quite a number wrote, and that was for me somehow the justification for the course.

In a letter to me, Professor Manasse tells the following stories:

In 1943 or 1944, I was approached by a friend who suggested that I should become a member of the "Southern Society for the Philosophy of Religion." This was a society of teachers of philosophy at mostly Southern colleges which met once a year, mostly at a hotel, for one or two days, at which papers relating to the philosophy of religion were read and discussed. I followed the suggestion and became formally a member of the society at a meeting in Chattanooga, Tennessee in 1944. (I read a paper on Franz Rosenzweig).

At the business session of that meeting it was discussed that it was desirable to invite black colleagues to become members of the up to that time entirely white organization. I at once thought of my colleague J. Neal Hughley, who was both a professor of economics or sociology at the North Carolina College for Negroes (the official name of the college which later became North Carolina Central University) and at the same time the college minister. He was a scholar and had a Ph.D. from Union Theological Seminary in New York. After talking to Mr. Hughley I nominated him for membership, but when the nominations for membership were presented at the business meeting of the following year (in Atlanta), Hughley's name was left out.

I was privately advised by one of the officers of the society that, contrary to what had appeared to be the consensus at the meeting of the preceding year, the officers had concluded that Negro colleagues should not be invited. I was told that as the meetings were usually held at hotels in the South and these hotels would not admit black guests, admitting them as members of the society would lead to something similar to "taxation without representation." Unfortunately I was not *schlagfertig* (German for quick-witted) to protest at once. But having returned to Durham, I wrote to the Secretary of the Society that I resigned my membership. At the same time, I wrote to two members whom I knew a little better, explaining the reasons for my resignation.

Several months later I got a letter from the Secretary informing me that the case had been discussed by several other members, that one had made a poll of the membership and it had appeared that the majority of the members had voted to invite Negroes to become members. I myself was asked that in view of this I should reconsider to remain (or to become a member again) and that one would now also invite Dr. Hughley to become a member. As the latter was ready to forget what had happened before and to accept the membership, I wrote to the Secretary that I now would remain (or become again) a member.

The next meeting was held at Black Mountain, North Carolina (not the College but a facility which, I believe, had been used for religious retreats). Both Hughley and I attended and there was still another black professor who had been nominated by somebody else. (I may add that at subsequent meetings I never felt well in the Society. I did not want to resign a second time but did not attend later meetings.) For a number of years I still paid my membership fees. I do not know if the Society still exists.

About the same time I had written an article with the title, "The Dance of the Latin Dance of Death," the manuscript of which I submitted to the periodical, *Medievalia et Humanistica*. I then was advised by my editor (who was a well known scholar, as I believe I remember at a Midwestern university) that the editorial board had decided to accept my manuscript for publication. But that it seemed to him (the editor) odd that I would name as my academic home the "North Carolina College for Negroes." Why not just print: "Durham, North Carolina?" As I remember it, I answered that when I was appointed to my position it was assumed that if I published scholarly papers, I would follow the custom to name the college at which I taught. This then was accepted and the paper appeared in 1946 with the name of the North Carolina College for Negroes attached to it. (Looking up a reprint of this paper which I still possess, I find that on the first page there is a note in which I express my thanks to John Hope Franklin "for many helpful suggestions".) All these were not world shattering events but I thought it would further illustrate the atmosphere in the academic world at that period.

I also interviewed Dr. Gabriel Manasse, the younger son, now a psychiatrist. His reminiscences follow:

I grew up in Durham. I lived there continuously from birth till I was 18. It was a quite strictly segregated Southern town and I grew up feeling very much an outsider. I was very embarrassed about the fact that my parents were Jewish, spoke with heavy German accents and taught at the black college. And all of that made me, at least in my own view, but I think also in reality, an outsider as far as the community was concerned.

There were very few Jews in my school or in my world. We were not very close to them, either. It also got problematic in other ways. My parents grew up in somewhat different circumstances. My mother, although Jewish by birth, was actually raised as a Christian, because her parents didn't want her to have the experience of discrimination which they had felt in Germany. And my father grew up in a small town in a farming area really, where his family celebrated actually both Jewish and Christian holidays. So, we grew up, my brother and I, with my family celebrating everything, and rather early on, we had a rather unpleasant experience when the local rabbi in Durham came to our house and we had a Christmas tree up. He was offended. I guess I must have been five or six, I don't know truly, but I know that that contributed to our isolation. I have a rather fragmentary memory of this, but that's how I understand the story, that we were not supposed to have a Christmas tree in our house.

Some people tried to start an integrated private school, but it was not possible then. Things were very, very strictly segregated and I know—and this I don't know from memory, but from actually quite recent conversations with my father and brother, that my parents could not have their black colleagues come to our house. They were threatened. I mean there were a host of incidents.

I remember very vividly an incident when I was with my mother on the bus. A pregnant black lady got on the bus and in those days blacks sat from the back forward and whites from front backward. And we were close to the place where those came together and there really were no other seats. And my mother—we had been in separate seats—picked me up and put me in her lap so that the black pregnant lady could sit down, which she did, at which point the bus driver stopped the bus and threw us off. That made an impression on me so that I remembered. I'm talking four, five, six years old, somewhere in there. Well, my mother was, in a certain sense, always a fighter. I mean she was angry and self-righteous. She was right, but—but in a battle that at that point of history could not be won.

So, there are those kinds of memories—and, and I had a fairly hostile attitude, I'd say, towards Jews, in general. I had no very close friends who were Jewish. There were some, but mostly my friends were not Jewish. I also know to this day, but then even more so, very, very little of the most basic things that everybody thinks that everybody knows about Judaism. I mean I didn't know such basic things as that Jews don't eat pork. Actually I think I remember more about my neighbors criticizing my family for being German than Jewish. They didn't seem to understand why we were there. This was after the war.

I didn't really know black people. My mother was particularly active in doing things. It's funny to say this again. But for instance, they had a big Christmas event every year at the college and I think my brother and I certainly often went with my mother to this. We'd sing German Christmas carols and things of that sort with the students that she was teaching German to. I speak German fluently, but with a lot of grammatical mistakes. At home we spoke a combination really.

We spoke about racism in terms of drinking fountains and bathrooms and waiting rooms and—I mean in hundreds of ways. To be completely honest, my sense is that the racism was so pervasive that I don't think that even my parents really understood it in the same sense one understands it today. It was such a way of life at that time that—I mean it was just everywhere, it was so thoroughly institutionalized.

We didn't, to my recollection, ever talk about it in school, although in fact I was there in my tenth grade when we got the very first integration in my high school, the very first. In fact, a lady whose father became quite prominent in a lot of stuff, Floyd McKissick, who became the president of CORE (Congress of Racial Equality). His daughter was in my tenth-grade class, the homeroom, and was the first black child—there may have been more than one, but she was among the first black children who were entered into the Durham high school.

The established good student leaders tended in Durham in that era to be relatively liberal, much more liberal than their parents were. And we tried very hard to make it a smooth event. Now there were some children who were very, very hostile to it. Actually, what I remember is one day, it could have been one of the first days, seeing some ink had been thrown on her dress and it was pretty awful. But there were several of us, and I was, by no means, in that sense, particularly noteworthy, who went out of our way to try to make it alright, you know, to try to welcome her and be nice and be decent. And actually, I think after a few days, in truth, there really was not much reaction, at least that I'm aware of.

My father was made the chairman of the Department of Latin, Greek and German, and of Philosophy, something made up, and my mother, then becoming a teacher of German, in fact worked under him, and that was, from his point of view at least, an extremely difficult situation to manage. Because my mother was and became increasingly, as she aged, pro-black, but pro-black in ways I'm not sure were always in their best interests if one looks in a longer scale. She wanted to be nice to the students and tended to give them perhaps better grades than they might have earned. She was I think quite popular with the coaches, the sports teams who always wanted their students—their athletes to go into her classes because they would almost invariably pass if they appeared. That made life extremely difficult for my father, who was conflicted about how to deal with this and really had no recourse. He tried for a long time to get German taken out from under his area, but unsuccessfully throughout his career.

Otherwise, in truth, I think in a certain sense, both were quite happy at the institution. My father in a more complex way I'd say, because—I think he is or was truly a scholar of a different type than that is feasible for a professor with lots of teaching duties in a relatively poor black college. So, his real life's work, in one sense, was quite undernourished in terms of that kind of development. On the other hand, I think he really did feel that the institution had, in effect, saved his life, and the life of his family, and I think he felt loyalty and went through a long period really of an unwillingness to go other places. I think in the latter years, that probably changed some and the circumstances, including my mother's willingness to go somewhere else, he might have. But I think for many years he would not have gone elsewhere. My mother was quite involved in a lot of things there, and she didn't really want to go to another institution.

I asked Dr. Manasse if his parents discussed the Nazi period with him and his brother when they were young. They went through very great unpleasantness in Italy, including Mrs. Manasse's incarceration with her new infant upon the insistence of the authorities, while Hitler was visiting Mussolini. His reply:

I don't know—in a certain sense, yeah. I mean, the outlines at least of what happened I think was discussed—was at least told. My father has to this day I think a lot of difficulty in discussing any of that. He very quickly gets distressed in his outlook and I think quickly lost in his thoughts and not communicative. Those things are so terrible to him to this day, that it remains very difficult for him to speak about it. My Mom, she probably talked a little bit more with me about it.

One of the happiest days of my life, I remember quite vividly, was the last day of school of I believe the fourth grade, when a photographer from the local newspaper in Durham, North Carolina, came to my school wanting to take a picture of children getting out for summer vacation. The newspaper wanted a picture of children getting out for the summer and they picked me because of my freckled face and whatnot and looking like the typical American child. I mean, it was the most wonderful thing that had ever happened to me that I got picked as the—I mean, it felt like I belonged.

Dr. Manasse doesn't remember if he told his parents.

Professor Kurt Braun taught at Howard University in Washington, D.C., from 1943 to 1969. I was fortunate to have the opportunity to interview his daughter, Ms. Susan Ripley. Some of her reminiscences follow:

Well, it was very much a time of segregation and it was certainly very much Virginia. Even Northern Virginia is very much Virginia. Well, by the time I was remembering things, it was very late 40s, early 50s, I went to a segregated school, I lived in a segregated neighborhood, the restaurants were segregated and my father's belief was that racial prejudice was taught, not inborn. And therefore, children who had any kind of racial prejudice had that because of something their parents had said or done or had taught them.

And one of the real early memories which must still have been the late 40s was when I was quite young, maybe three, my father had people from the university over for a dinner party and I was allowed to stay up a little while and pass around the hors d'oeuvres. And he had insisted that nobody mention the fact that the guests were going to be black, because his theory was that if you didn't point that out, children would not make a distinction. My mother was worried about that particular philosophy and so was my grandmother.

At any rate, the evening came and I was passing around the hors d'oeuvres and, as the story goes, I stopped in front of a woman who was the head of the classics department and looked at her for a minute and then said, "are you a maid?" And my mother and my grandmother were absolutely horrified and she, thank goodness, just seemed to be mildly amused and said, "no, dear, I'm head of the classics department." But my father at that point realized that children, in fact, do observe racial differences. They may not make a value judgment, but they certainly notice. I don't remember this very well.

I remember people coming to the house and what I remember of people coming to the house was more the reaction of the neighbors. My whole frame of reference was that anyone who was black was a maid or a garbage collector or someone like that because there wasn't any other black person that I saw at that point. I had a very high regard for maids, but I just didn't know anyone else. When these people would come to our house, the neighbors and especially a neighbor two doors up who was from Georgia was always utterly horrified that we were allowing these people in our house and having dinner with them. And that made quite an impression on me.

When I started school, I know that—that it was quite a thing for the other kids that my father taught in a school that was all "Negroes." And what you have to remember is that even as late as I graduated from high school, which was 1963, we still had almost completely segregated school systems.

My father would take me down to the university with him sometimes so that I was exposed to people other than maids and garbage collectors. But other than that, in my own life there were certainly no black kids, no integration in anything I did because it didn't exist in Virginia and we lived in Virginia.

He was very liberal and he—one of the other things I remember is that during some of the first major demonstrations in town, when Martin Luther King spoke at the Lincoln Memorial, and that was 1963, and there was an enormous gathering in town and I wanted to go down. By that time I was 17 and I was determined to go and my mother, who was terrified of large gatherings, I think still left over from Berlin and the

Nazis and a riot was a riot was a riot, absolutely forbade that I go down there.

And my father came home from work that evening and said, well, he went down to the Mall, and my mother was so shocked. And he had gone to the Lincoln Memorial and heard Martin Luther King speak there and had said that he felt that Martin Luther King was probably the most powerful speaker he had ever heard in his life. That while he may take exception with some of his remarks, by and large, he was nonetheless the most influential man and—the power of his speech was just amazing. I can remember him going down after major racial unrest in Washington during the "Burn baby burn" phase of the period he had gone into his classroom and written "Learn baby learn" on the blackboard and was having nothing to do with it.

He was very distressed that the whole racial thing was taking a kind of a destructive direction and certainly upset that it existed on the campus. And there were bomb threats and all kinds of things like that that were going on, all of which he completely disregarded. They would have regular bomb threats and the buildings would have to be emptied and it was a means of disrupting class, and he would refuse to leave the building, he would continue to talk. And he told his students this is scare techniques, some people are trying to disrupt us and the most important thing you can do is continue your education. You can't give in to these people.

He was very brave and a very principled man and he said these are cowards, they're not going to blow up the building and I'm not going to leave and I'm not going to buy into this, and he would continue to teach. And if any student wanted to leave, that was his business, but my father would continue to teach and he would not disrupt the class or hold it later.

One of the incidents that happened toward the end of his teaching career there was, that he was driving on to the campus one day and a student lay down in the middle of the road in an effort to bar him from coming on to campus. I'm not sure that the student objected to the fact that my father was white, so much as that it was part of the whole disruption of classes that was going on. The whole closing of the university.

(This was a boycott, like many at that period on black as well as white campuses, with the objective of changing the prevailing educational system into what the students perceived to be a more just and "relevant" one. GSE)

My father leaned out the window and said to him, "I'm not stopping, you're going to have to move. And if you don't move, I will run over you," which the student didn't believe and my father did not stop. And at the last moment, the student jumped out of the road—my father never stopped—at which point he pressed charges for assault with a deadly weapon, meaning the car, and it went to a hearing. It never went to trial, but it did go to a hearing. My father at that time was about 70 and the student was young and very strong, a large man, and the judge dismissed it as absurd. "People who lie down in the middle of the road in front of cars are taking a certain degree of chance themselves."

But I think that his career there ended on a somewhat bitter note because of all the boycotts and riots and because he was so dedicated to the education of all people and that equality came through education and that this whole disruption of the educational system was such a great error. He didn't stop teaching, incidentally. He then went on to Catholic University and taught there.

My parents attended plenty of receptions and parties, I mean there was a great deal of university socializing and some private socializing. I didn't get to know any of their friends' children because they'd come to dinner without their children. At one point one of his students baby-sat for me, I do recall that.

My father talked a lot about the disastrous effects of prejudice and the problems that came about from prejudice. And one of the interesting correlates was that he was very open to the Germans, which my mother was never open to. She never wanted to go back to Germany. She was not comfortable traveling, visiting, anything, wanted to have nothing to do with Germans. And my father's point was that they should not discuss that in front of me because it was continuing a prejudice that had nothing to do with me and that I was born after that time and any Germans that I knew or became friends with would probably be my age and would have been born after that time and that to continue that kind of hatred into the next generation was criminal.

And I think a lot of that carried over to my attitude to all racial minorities, that slavery was slavery, but I'm now and my relationship with people of other races and predominantly blacks is the very twentieth century and it has no bearing on the history of it, not to say that the history is to be ignored, but that our relationships have to be based on our lives and not disputes that our parents had. Because I had been taught that it was wrong for me to hate the Germans because of what they did to my parents, my grandparents, or aunts or uncles or anything else, which was quite an approach for my father, who lost his entire family. He was the only survivor in his entire family. A couple of members in my mother's family survived, none in my father's. And yet, I was always taught that that was not my fight and that it would be sinful for me to continue to have that attitude because those people were not the ones that I was dealing with and that their children could not be held responsible for their actions any more than I could be, and that it would be the same for those children to continue the hatred against the Jews as for me to continue the hatred against Germans.

I don't recall him saying anything specifically correlating the two events (the fate of the blacks and the Jews), but he had a real violent hatred of segregation of any kind. I mean, he approved of the fact that Howard was there because it was necessary, but he was basically very pro-integration and certainly, within the school system that I went to, very pro-integration.

There were people in the neighborhood, and he was a part of that—who, when integration was first being mentioned, one of the concerns was—in the part of Virginia that I was from, the integration started at the high schools and worked down, which was somewhat illogical, but at any rate, that's how they did it. And the concern was that the kids who would be entering the high schools would not have had as broad an education as the kids already there, and so they were going to start at a disadvantage. And a lot of the segregationists I think regarded that as a great plus and it may have been part of the reason for starting it in high school was to show that these kids couldn't possibly keep up. And he was involved in a group who took on the tutoring of these kids to see to it that when they came into the school, they could hold their own and that there wouldn't be problems like that.

The integration that took place was—I think three kids entered our school and that was it. Their football fields were back to back, they were that close, but we were told, well, there just weren't any black kids in our jurisdiction, which was somewhat absurd. And he was very violent on that whole subject of segregation and very much against it, but I don't recall any particular conversations of saying that this was related to what happened to the Jews.

At this point Mr. Scott Ripley, Ms. Susan Braun Ripley's husband, who had been present at the interview, asked if he might add something, and of course I welcomed his joining in:

Kurt Braun's understanding of the black experience in America and the experience of the Jews in Germany—I think on one level there was an obvious affinity, he could appreciate a parallel between the two. On the other hand, what was very striking to me was that Kurt almost belittled his own suffering at the hands of the Germans and his own problems compared to the people who suffered terminally and died in the camps. And I think on one level, he had tremendous understanding for the blacks; on another level, nothing really compared in his mind with the suffering of people who remained in Germany and suffered the final solution of the Nazis.

His own troubles, his own experiences, he never chose to write about after great encouragement from Susan and myself and other people, who found that the stories he told us about his experiences we thought enormously important and they deserved to be written about. He was so much in awe of the horror that others had experienced that he never felt that he could write that and I honestly think that while sympathy was there and he could identify very clearly with the blacks here in this country, I think that the experience of the blacks here in this country, in his mind, paled beside the experience of the Jews in Germany.

But one of the things that I also found interesting is that in dealing later in his life, particularly when he was ill and his wife was ill and there were suddenly numbers of uneducated black women and men who were taking care of them, what tremendous respect he had for these uneducated black people, that there was a respect for the suffering, it sounds terribly corny, but the souls of these people.

The neighborhood that they lived in, it's an affluent suburb of Washington, but it was more than that. It wasn't just well-to-do merchants. I mean, the neighborhood was almost entirely high ranking military officers, important foreign service officers, civil servants. I mean, it was a very Washington neighborhood, almost like Georgetown, Georgetown with families is what it amounts to. Georgetown with children. And they underwent a great deal of pressure and prejudice for having "fancy niggers" in their house; that's the phrase that was used in the neighborhood; that the president of Howard University or the dean of the law school was visiting. And I mean there was pressure which some native born people probably would have taken very seriously, which Kurt and his wife dusted off their shoulders and absolutely ignored.

Professor Erna Magnus taught in the School of Social Work at Howard University from 1947 to 1966. Upon applying for an apartment, she was asked if she ever entertained colleagues or students at home. When she replied affirmatively, her application was turned down.

Professor John Herz, who taught political science at Howard 1941–1943 and 1948–52, initially lived near the campus. Here is what he told:

We settled down in Washington (1941)—Washington, of course, segregated at that time—close to the campus, but in a street which was still white and closed. A strange thing that happened at that time was that where we were living there in a second floor of a two-story house, one house in that street was sold to a black family. And that meant, as you know, that the whole street, everybody got out, the whites got out and blacks took over. We thought that since I was teaching at Howard University, I didn't have or we shouldn't have reason to leave, too. And so, we stayed when the house was bought by a black man and they moved in, in the downstairs and we stayed upstairs. But then we noticed something strange, which at first we hadn't thought of. We were rather thoughtless maybe, namely that the blacks who had "conquered" the

street resented that we lived there, thus taking an apartment away from
one of theirs. And so we noticed that and we moved away at that time.
No, it was never said. It may—it was our impression. It may be a wrong
impression. We were uncomfortable in that sense and then we moved
elsewhere. So we lived for a while very close to the campus. We made
good friends with colleagues at Howard, of course mostly black ones.

One impression I had or one thing which impressed me very much was
that I had first thought it would be a very strange thing for me to face
this sea of black faces of students. But after a short while, I didn't see
that anymore. I became, so to speak, colorblind. There were no white
students among the undergraduates. But once I asked a student, "aren't
there any white students here?" and he said, "no, only a few Jews at the
medical school," which impressed me very much. In other words, there
were some white students at (black) medical schools because you had this
numerus clausus (quota) in many medical schools, especially for Jews, and
so Jews went to that school.

There was one thing that was explained to me right away, namely when
we came over and came to Howard, that there was a certain amount of
traditional anti-Semitism in some black quarters for a very specific reason,
namely that especially in cities like New York or so, and—and the lower
class, poor Negroes would meet Jews in the form of management of their
housing, for instance, the owner. Also sometimes stores and so on. And
so, they felt exploited by them or had difficulties with them and that
created animosity. But that was nothing that we noticed—maybe with
that one exception of what I told you about our apartment. That might
have had something to do with that too. But we were on good relations
with the owners of that house, for instance. Never any difficulty there.

One of the central themes in this work is the interaction between the
refugees and the African Americans where members of both groups
articulate to each other their respective histories of persecution, oppression and terror. It may seem incomprehensible in retrospect, but I have
found hardly any instances where there was talk about this tragic history, let alone any mention of a sense of common destiny, different as
its origins and manifestations were, and are. This silence can be understood in several ways. At that period of time, there was little public
discussion of the extermination camps, or of African American history,
compared to later years. Perhaps even more significant, there was an
understandable reluctance to share the experience of suffering and
shame one had undergone, with relative strangers who could not be
expected to understand the "other" world. One only talked about these
horrors among one's selves, where one is assured of understanding.

A notable and very affecting exception to this situation took place between John Biggers and Viktor Lowenfeld. Biggers was a scholarship student at Hampton, then Institute, now University, from Gastonia, North Carolina. Lowenfeld, a refugee from Vienna, was head of the Art Department at Hampton. He had found a Department of Industrial Arts upon his arrival and changed it to an Art Department in the conviction that anyone with the talent and the interest could become an artist and did not have to be limited to carrying out others' designs. Biggers has become a major figure as a painter, and at the time of the following interview was "1988 Texas Artist of the Year." He tells the story this way:

> That was one experience I'll never forget. Sometimes we would work late in the Art Department and—and if you missed your dinner in the dining room—we didn't have any money, we didn't have anything to eat. So Viktor sometimes would say, "well, come on, you can get a sandwich at my house." But driving across the campus, he would always stop at the post office. Then he would drive that little beautiful road around the waterfront where he lived on the campus.
> This particular day when he stopped and got the mail and he kind of came out, he was ghostly white. And he didn't say one word. He got in the car and he drove, but he stopped there near the water's edge and he pulled the letter out and read it to me. He had gotten it from the State Department. And in this letter, they were telling him, informing him of some of his folks that they had discovered were burned in the—in one of those camps. Now this was—this was one of the—again one of the most horrendous experiences I've ever had because a human being was telling me that his family—and he named them—were victims; they had been burned. But this was a terrifying kind of experience. And I had heard of neighbors whose—members of their families had been lynched. But I realized that race and color might not have any meaning at all when it comes to terrifying experiences in this world.
> So, because of this horrendous experience, however vicarious, I always felt a relationship with Viktor because he had shared this with me. I felt the relationship had truly crossed all country and racial barriers, so that— those barriers were crossed now. That was no longer a part of the struggle to understand a person and to communicate with a person.

Professor John Herz also expressed himself in this context, albeit not as dramatically, and from a refugee's perspective, when asked about it:

> That's a very good and important question and that was really the—the main—for me, the main you might call it emotional experience which I had, that here were people with whom I could empathize because they

were also victims of racial policies and racial persecution. And I think
that especially in the case of Ralph Bunche, that established right away
a bond. (Bunche was then chairman of the Political Science department
at Howard.) Because Bunche had that feeling that these German refugees,
Jews and others were—especially Jews because of so-called racial persecution, racial policies of Hitler—were—there was something which—
which—how you say—make them close to their own experience and their
own fate. They were discriminated here in this country and—as we were
or had been in—in Europe, and that established a something which I am
very sad that at this point it has changed so much.

Upon being asked if this was ever discussed with his students, Herz
said:

Yes. yes. Sure. Sure. That was discussed all the time, whether I have a
course in political theory or international relations, international politics,
and so on. For instance, well, what's going on there, and Hitler, what is
that kind of persecution, what does he have against Jews, how come and
that whole racial theory, and so on, and that was the basis for our
discussion. And I noticed right away that they, from their viewpoint, were
as much interested in that kind of problem as were we refugees. And I
mentioned Bunche, above all, but also other colleagues developed this
right away as—a certain sympathy to us as victims of racial persecution,
which they knew all about.

An important and probably not uncommon contrast is presented in
the interview with George Carter:

I started at Lincoln in 1946, after 2 1/2 years in the Army (in Europe),
as a sophomore. It was my intention to major in philosophy. One of the
first persons I met on the faculty was a German by the name of Fales,
Walter Fales. I probably took more courses and spent more time with Dr.
Fales over the course of the next three years than with any other single
faculty member. I was not aware for a good part of the beginning of my
relationship with him that he was Jewish. I thought of him as German.
He was German in every sense of the word. His—his thinking, his thought
patterns, his culture, his attitude was that of a—of a German. I'm not
sure what the incident was which made me aware of the fact that he was
Jewish. But one day I learned that his former name was Feilchenfeld. And
I really cannot remember, but it was at that point that I realized that he
had—that he was a German Jewish refugee.
    I really can't speak to anything significant of—as to how I saw Walter
Fales as a Jewish, German Jewish refugee in this country. I did not experience him as such. It was late in my relationship with him that I

realized he was Jewish. I suppose, if I were really to do a lot of introspection, I would say a lot about myself and the fact that I was just not sensitive to this at all. I saw him as a—as a mentor, as a very brilliant person, as a person who had a great deal to teach me in a field that I'd chosen to major in. His impact as a teacher on me was monumental.

It was interesting to watch Fales, as I began to do, adjust to living in a black world. I found him at times doing things and saying things which he just shouldn't have been doing and saying in that community. And on a couple of occasions, I took him aside and said, "hey look, you don't do that here." In one of my classes he was talking about cultural differences and he referred to another class of his, where there were many more students, and he talked about the odor of the students and he did that very innocently. That bunch of guys smell, different from anybody—different from a group—any other group.

And I remember a couple of days later, after a class, closing in to him and saying, "hey, look, be careful, don't do that. Your motivation, your interest, your curiosity is very real; it will not be taken this way. You're dealing with a group of young black males in the middle of the twentieth century and they're not ready to have a white European tell them that they smell bad, and that's what they're hearing." And then we had a discussion why people smell differently. You fly into Dakar, West Africa, on a hot day and you get off the plane and it smells different from flying into Bombay, India, and that smells different from Rome, Italy, and it's all because of what people eat and their bathing—a whole bunch of things.

I found him very, very curious about the complexion of the women that the students were involved with. Lincoln was an all-black—well, there were four or five white students there, but for all practical purposes, it was an all-black, all-male school. It's 50, 60 miles from Philadelphia. It's very isolated. The only women there were the wives and daughters of faculty members and staff people. On occasions of football games, big campus events, women would come out in busloads from all kinds of places. And I remember one football afternoon I was walking with him somewhere and he saw a student whom he had gotten to know well and he was somewhat clumsy. And I asked him a couple of questions after that and I got the sense that he was interested in the whole phenomenon of what complexion Negro women the various fellows had out there as girlfriends.

We are talking now about the late 40s, when the whole dynamic of shades of color had a very different impact within the black community than they do today. My children, either of my children, they don't have anything like the kind of baggage that we carried around. You know, you don't have to be a German Jewish refugee to respond to that. I think that this is something of a curiosity for Europeans, in general, if not American whites who live apart from black communities.

I think it is probably true that Fales was one of the first whites whom

I got to know on a long-term intimate basis. And I say that rather, somewhat, guardedly, because I grew up in an integrated neighborhood in Philadelphia. I went to integrated schools. The whites were not nearly as foreign to me as to many other people who came to Lincoln, came out of the deep South, as most of them did. But I would guess that I got to learn more about white thinking about blacks as I observed Fales, heard him talk about this. I guess that's true.

He fit into the environment very well. He fit kind of a stereotype of our culture, in the American culture. Fales was a small man, kind of frail, almost delicate. He was the crazy, professorial poet in the minds of most. "Yeah, he's a great guy, but geez, you know—" I have a picture somewhere of Fales with a tennis racket and he's leaping up in the air trying to hit it and he's about the most unathletic person imaginable. But society tolerates people like that, but it also kind of smiles at them. Lincoln's values were very, very different from those that he represented.

I have related a number of stories told by the scholars and other witnesses to illustrate the central character of race in black-white relations as they prevailed in those times and places, with special meaning for the exceptional situation of the refugees with respect to race. Here are some more instances, this one found in a summary Dr. Eric Fischer wrote about his life in the United States, sent to me by his son.

Dr. Fischer, a geographer from Vienna, taught the Army in Europe during the occupation, joined OSS, the State Department, and thereafter began his career in academic institutions, initially at the Geographic Research Institute at the University of Virginia. Later he taught at NYU, but during the Korean War was hired by the Army Map Service. He did some teaching at George Washington and Catholic University. After retiring from government service in 1965, he became professor of geography at Coppin State College in Baltimore, Maryland, until his mandatory retirement at seventy, when he continued to do some teaching at Montgomery College in Takoma Park, Maryland. Coppin State was in a poor black neighborhood of Baltimore, and most of the students came from families and schools which had not provided the students with much background for college work, certainly not in geography, never a subject well taught in most public schools. Fischer comments that he found this a challenge and an opportunity for the teacher; he perceived his students as people intent on gaining an education in order to improve their lot in the world. He got along well with the black faculty, but does not comment on any social relations outside the college. Here is a story as told by Dr. Fischer:

> There was a tall, never smiling young man in my freshman class, apparently slightly older than the average high school graduate. In general, the boys clustered in the last rows except a few who sat with the girls. This young man sat alone in the middle of the first row. The seats behind him were left empty. He was unusual in wearing jewelry such as bracelets, earrings. He was an excellent student. Once a girl explained his strange ways to me: he is a Black Muslim. At the time Black Muslims were not well known among whites and shunned by other blacks.
>   One day, he came to class with a swastika dangling from a necklace. First I did not know how to react. Then I used the opportunity that another student went to the wall map to explain something, leaving me time to approach the offender, conveniently seated in his isolated first row seat. I whispered: "Do you know that I am Jewish and what the swastika means to me?" He looked up but said no word. For the rest of the hour I paid no attention to him. He never again came to class with his "ornament." These four years at Coppin did both, widen my understanding for the black people and giving me a feeling that my activity was of help.

A letter from the American Friends Service Committee of 1944 to President Thomas Jones of Fisk University contains the only reference of its kind I have found in the archival material at my disposal:

> . . . Dr. Fromm (not further identified) has raised the question of the possibility of placement of refugees in a colored institution and [. . .] I have advised him that, in general, we do not recommend the placement of refugees in these institutions because of the double handicap it places them under . . .

It is the only example I have found on the part of a placement agency which mentions the thought-provoking phrase "double handicap" as a factor in the matter of refugee adjustment to the new environment.

Professor Joseph Herbert Furth from Vienna taught economics and sociology at Lincoln University from 1939–1944. After applying for a position there, letters were sent to a number of scholars asking for references. Among the questions asked, there was one concerning the applicant's position on teaching in a black institution. Furth, aware of the question, replied in a letter to Professor Oskar Morgenstern, then at Princeton (in German, my translation):

I would of course be delighted if I could get the position at Lincoln; a halfway intelligent individual of Jewish descent, who went through six months in Nazi Austria, must have sufficient interest in and understanding of the Negro question.

"Double handicap" is evidently an apt phrase to illustrate the handicap of being a Jewish refugee teaching in a black college.

From Fisk University, we have correspondence with Theodore Wilhelm Danzel of January 17, 1935, from Hamburg, addressed to President Jones. He wants to accept a teaching position at Fisk in ethnology. In the end, the matching grant required by the Emergency Committee did not materialize, and Danzel never taught at Fisk. Here is a quote from Danzel's letter, which illustrates how little some of these Europeans knew of the racial situation in the United States and about African Americans at the time:

Since my youth I made coloured people my particular occupation, either by investigating as an ethnologist the monuments of pre-European time, or more directly by teaching their members some of the knowledge which they can use in their evolution. So I did teaching in China, so I did investigating among the Indians of Mexico. I assure you my warmest interest and sympathy in your work.

It is not altogether clear how the matching fund problem caused Danzel's rejection; it might have been a decision by Fisk not to apply, for reasons unknown from the available documents.

The President of West Virginia State College, Dr. John W. Davis, wrote the following letter to the Emergency Committee in 1939:

I appreciate the attention which you have so kindly given my letter of June 24th which treats the subject of our need of a refugee scholar in romance philology. Very particularly, we would want this worker to be able to teach German, Spanish and French. Naturally, he must have a speaking and working knowledge of English for the best success here. It is not necessary that he know Italian. The working staff of this college is composed largely of Negroes. However, we used in a successful study last year with Ohio State University fourteen white persons of the staff of Ohio State.

The enclosed special announcement which treats special courses for teachers of the deaf and blind shows a use of white instructors only. The persons who are offering special courses for the teachers of the deaf and the blind are now here. Thus far this summer, we have had six or eight teachers from Ohio State University working in our summer session. Legally, then, our staff is composed of Negroes. Factually and rightly, our staff is composed of Whites and Negroes.

In West Virginia we have very little trouble with the so-called race problem. We work here as an accredited college in which the search for truth and cooperative understanding among races and nations forms the dominant tone. The scholar we need would not meet undesirable prejudices here which would offset constructive educational efforts. It is my hope that you will be able to name for us an acceptable scholar for our work in romance philology. I hope that the statement herein will satisfy the point of the question in your letter of July 8th. Let me hear from you.

Frederick Lehner and his wife, Stella were at West Virginia State College from 1939 until their death in 1961. In 1940 Lehner reported to the Emergency Committee on his first term at the college. The following is the paraphrase from the Committee:

The West Virginia State College is a negro institution. The President received him enthusiastically, and the faculty, he says, has been kindness itself. He has been made conscious of no race problem, although he and his wife are the only white members of the college community. The College pleases Dr. Lehner very much. He wrote us once about its atmosphere of "scholarly happiness," and he enjoys his students greatly. The surrounding country reminds him of the Vienna Woods, and he and his wife go "mountain-climbing" on Sundays.

They live on the campus. No one has treated the Lehners as outsiders and it distresses him that his negro associates are barred from attending theatres, concerts, or movies with him in the nearby white community. (The campus has its own hall, where movies and occasional concerts are given.) Several faculty members invited him to drive with them to the Modern Language Association convention in New Orleans. Although he was anxious to attend that conference, he declined, for he knew that he and his hosts would have had to put up in different hotels in New Orleans.

Incidentally, he finds plenty of material for sociological study. In addition to the $900 subscribed jointly by the Oberlaender Trust and the Emergency Committee, Dr. Lehner is given his board and the use of several rooms in a dormitory. His wife volunteers her services in the college library. The College's regular language teachers have been shifted to the teaching of Spanish as a result of renewed interest in Latin-American relations, and Dr. Lehner has fallen heir to all the French and German classes.

The President of the College has been so pleased to have Dr. Lehner this year that he wants to take him on a trip among the neighboring negro colleges to draw attention to the availability of other foreign scholars. This will not be practicable, however, unless the President can mention the possibility of securing grants from our organization and similar groups, for the colleges are poor. Dr. Lehner wanted to know what he might tell the President.

In 1963, Stella Lehner's *Viennese Cookings* was published by the college, to be sold for $1 to provide additional funds from its sale to supplement the "Doctor Frederick Lehner Loan and Scholarship Fund" at the college.

From the great centers of learning in Europe—To the quiet campus of West Virginia State College—Dr. Lehner made the transition readily. For he was a scholar unfettered by the narrow confines of countries, colors or creeds. Thus it was, Frederick Lehner became the first white professor on the staff of this distinguished Negro college. To live in the hearts of men is not to die.

This little tribute was printed in the 1964 college Bulletin in memory of the Lehners.

Dr. Katherine Radke was the director of the Xavier University School of Social Service from 1935–1938. I have only one document concerning her work at Xavier which, however, is significant. It is addressed to the New Orleans branch of the NAACP, to bring to their attention that,

The Department of Public Welfare of the city of New Orleans has cut off relief rolls a certain percentage of colored clients and has started to discriminate considerably against those Negroes who have been kept on the relief rolls.

Dr. Radke goes into precise detail describing and analyzing the new ruling and concludes by writing:

In order to clarify this issue and in order to try to stop the slow starvation of a large section of the population by all means available I would appreciate your cooperation in sending protests to the persons given on Appendix II. It is very desirable to lodge your and your organization's protest with them as quickly as possible.

In 1937, in Louisiana, a protest and collaboration with the NAACP by a foreign professor was a remarkable act.

CHAPTER 6

The Pursuit of Happiness

The Emergency Committee in Aid of Displaced Foreign Scholars began its operations soon after the Nazi takeover, in 1933. After the end of the War in Europe, it was decided to disband the Committee formally as of June 1, 1945. It was also decided to prepare a history of the Committee's work, which appeared in 1948 under the title, *The Rescue of Science and Learning*, and was prepared by the two most active officers over the years, Stephen Duggan and Betty Drury, chairman and executive secretary, respectively. This little volume contains a number of observations useful to this study. While there is but one reference to the African American connection, there are a number of observations of interest regarding refugee scholars and their adjustment to the social and educational situation they found themselves in which are applicable to the scholars in this work. There is an evocative point made in the foreword which relates directly to an observation made earlier:

> . . . the unwillingness of scholars to bare their lives lest they appear as applicants for charity; their hesitancy to tell all the facts about their circumstances because of fear of reprisals to loved ones at home; reluctance to describe candidly their experiences in their college environment here lest they be considered guilty of ingratitude.[1]

Included in the publication are two questionnaires sent to refugee scholars and college administrators, respectively, as well as a number of responses received. The questions for the scholars were:

1. Were you happy during your stay in an American institution of higher learning?

2. Were the members of the college faculty, administration, and students kindly disposed?

3. Do you think you rendered a real service, and if so of what nature?

4. Have you any general comments you would like to share with us?[2]

All individuals and institutions remained anonymous in this report. The only reference to a "Southern Negro institution" reads as follows:

> I was happy to work and live with American Negroes and found the faculty members, the administration, and the students extremely pleasant. I formed lasting friendships. . . . The faculty consisted of a group of fine scholars, many of them with an international background. The interest for true scholarship was encouraging, the understanding of minority problems proved comforting. . . . Needless to stress that there was not the slightest friction or misunderstanding because of "race, creed, or color."[3]

Another response, while not mentioning race, might well have come from a scholar in a historically black college:

> Although we were very kindly received by some members of the faculty, we felt from the beginning that we did not quite fit into the framework of a conservative, provincial, small college which stresses religion and abstinence, teaching and conformity to 'the powers that be' at the expense of scholarship and variety of interests, of cosmopolitanism and originality.[4]

I quote this following response because it is so typical of a European reaction to a very American concept:

> Was I happy during my stay?—Very, very much, from the first day to the present day. . . . Even now it strikes me as wonderful that a questionnaire asks me whether I am *happy*; I don't believe that could happen anywhere in the world except in this country.[5]

In what other nation is "The Pursuit of Happiness" enshrined in a founding document?

A comment by the authors shed light on a considerable problem encountered among Europeans:

> Some European professors whose academic career had been spent at a university of international fame dreaded loss of prestige if they entered

upon American teaching life in rural or suburban colleges. In European countries education is divided into three categories: elementary, secondary, and university. In the United States there are four divisions, the college being interposed between the secondary school and the university. Many Europeans failed to understand the honorable status enjoyed by the college in the American world of higher education. Anxiety was frequently expressed lest library facilities in the smaller institutions might not prove adequate—a doubt that closer acquaintance with the American scene often dispelled.[6]

I must add to this sanguine comment that first, most historically black colleges were "colleges," not universities, which did not offer Ph.D.s until 1957, when Howard University graduated its first doctoral students. Several black colleges did have medical, dental and theological schools, including Howard, which was called University from early on. Secondly, of course some of the small colleges did indeed have difficulty maintaining adequate libraries.

This account would be incomplete if it did not take note of the fact that the professors were not all equipped with the use of faultless English. Many had to study English before accepting any teaching positions; others spoke haltingly, and most with a heavy accent. Here is one reply to the questionnaire:

In contrast to most European colleges and universities where the relationship between the professor and the students is characterized by the hierarchic attitude of the former, the American student's relationship to his teacher is marked by a spirit of democracy. The respect of the student for the teacher here in this country, doesn't imbue him with shyness, and he feels completely free in discussions in the classroom. That I never experienced any sarcasm on account of my shortcomings in English speech or foreign accent, I consider a result of the same democratic practice.[7]

Naturally, the terror in Europe affected many refugee scholars deeply for many years. This comment is eloquent:

The years have, naturally, been difficult ones. In addition to the necessity of an adjustment to a new environment, new methods of teaching, and new material, the development in Europe has influenced us greatly, as the father of my wife was deported by the Nazis and as we did not hear from him (he died in the camp) and other members of our families for years.[8]

The report continues:

> Certain scholars lost all track of wives and children, and went on year
> after year with no sure knowledge of whether they lived or had perished.
> To some among them, a long period of uncertainty was terminated by a
> report of the extermination of those nearest and dearest to them.[9]

The questions put to the school administrators, as follows:

1. Were the displaced scholars in your institution readily absorbed?

2. Did they provide a problem, and if so what was its nature?

3. Did they make a scholarly contribution to the institution, and if so
   of what kind?

4. Have you any general comments?[10]

Some observations follow:

> What has impressed me most is not the difficulty which the Germans in
> particular have in adapting their Teutonic background and experience to
> the American undergraduate scene ... but their success in making the
> adjustment. It has provided a great diversity of points of view, and it has
> brought to us many men of distinction.[11]

And, from another institution:

> The chief difficulty, apart from personality problems, in adjusting dis-
> placed scholars has been of course to get them to understand that the
> American college is neither Gymnasium (lycee, liceo) on the one hand,
> nor a continental university on the other. But once more, if they are not
> afflicted with arrogance, they seem very quickly to understand the dis-
> tinctive octave of values within which we sing our song, and to join
> harmoniously in the chorus.[12]

The word "arrogant" appears from time to time, not surprisingly,
when one considers the exalted position professors held in Germany.
Of another order is the following remark of a displaced scholar from
a small college in a midwestern state:

> In my work I have, so far, not had any difficulties apart from a slight
> complaint concerning allegedly "radical" views in political economy. It

was reported to me—in the way of a subtle "hint"—that unfortunately many colleges have had the experience that the refugee professor did not seem to have sympathy with the American system of free enterprise, and that consequently most of them had transferred such professors from the Social Science Department of their respective schools to the Language Department.[13]

This observation leads me to several points in the matter of the American fear of radicalism of the left. A number of the refugees were certainly social democrats in Germany, a party well to the left of the American Democratic Party, but not identified with communism. During the anti-communist witchhunts before the War, suspended during the U.S.-U.S.S.R. alliance and resumed at the beginning of the cold war in 1947, the universities became a target for the Congressional and State investigating committees. Loyalty oaths and other tests were used which caused much upheaval in the academies. In her book, *No Ivory Tower: McCarthyism and the Universities*, Ellen W. Schrecker of Yeshiva University has given a thoroughly researched account of this historical episode. In the chapter describing the recourse the ousted scholars had for employment, she observes:

Teaching jobs did exist. Though it was all but impossible for the black-listed professors to get regular academic appointments at a mainstream college or university, they could sometimes find positions in the periphery. . . . To get such a job, a fulltime tenure track position in an American college, a blacklisted professor would have to go to the South, to the small, poor, denominational Negro colleges that were so desperate for qualified faculty members that they would hire anybody with a Ph.D. including teachers other educational institutions dared not touch. Only a few people exercised this option. The teaching conditions at such schools were depressing; academic standards were low; and professors rarely had the luxury of teaching courses in their own fields. In addition, life in the segregated South was not very attractive to a northern radical.[14]

As we have learned, this evaluation of the black colleges by no means tells the whole story about these institutions, but Professor Schrecker is making a generalization prevalent in white academic circles. In my study, one refugee scholar encountered a problem with the political climate of the fifties and the near paranoic fear of educational institutions to be painted and tainted with the red brush. In this instance, it was Talladega College which refused Fritz Pappenheim tenure in a really dramatic scene, as told by Jim McWilliams, a student there at that time:

During my second year, a controversy developed in which Dr. Pappenheim, who was very, very popular, had been told that he could not receive tenure at the school. And we were informed that it was because the school was going to begin teaching bread and butter courses like money and banking, and statistics and things that would be very useful to up-and-coming blacks. Now we younger students suspected that that was baloney. The older students sort of knew that that was baloney. And Professor Pappenheim merely said in his defense that getting a doctorate in economics from Heidelberg probably prepared him for money and banking, if that was what they wanted him to teach.

But the underlying reason I think is that this school, as isolated as it was, away from the mainstream of the day, of McCarthyism, was being affected. And the real reason was that Pappenheim refused to answer whether he was a communist or not. He didn't think it was their business and they—the Board of Trustees—felt strongly that he should have answered that and he would not answer it. And [. . .] the students heard that they had decided to deny him tenure, and that it would be his last year—we found this out while they were attending a meeting in the gymnasium—

In the South in those days, where there was no air-conditioning, and the temperature was maybe 98°. It began to get hot in May. And for some strange reason, the board of trustees could not get out of the building. Someone had locked all the doors and the windows. And the New York banking set, in their flannel suits, began to falter in the heat. And when they asked what would be the concessions for getting out, because this was 1952, long before Berkeley and other places, and so no one knew what might happen.

This board was primarily white. And they had church people. And when the people on the inside began to slip notes out and asking what would be a compromise, we met and agreed that the compromise would have to be a one-for-one. If Pappenheim went, the president would have to go. That was the Reverend Adam Daniel Beittel, a white man. There had not been a black president up until then. And after some sweating, they agreed, and so Mr. Beittel was let go.

We had no idea that this was unusual, revolutionary or whatever, because we were isolated in a small school, just tending to books. Well, Beittel left and several other professors who had not liked what had happened to Pappenheim resigned, very fine professors. There was talk that Pappenheim began his economics course with the *Communist Manifesto*. I don't think he began with that. Remember, he was a theoretician and a scholar, so the *Manifesto* would have come much later. He would have used *Das Kapital*, the Marx explanation of economics, as well as some Americans, and Adam Smith, and all that. Pappenheim did not approach scholarship with indoctrination, but exposure and analysis, and confront you with the options and whether you could defend your position. And had an interest in developing a curiosity so that he said you'd have the rest of your life to fill in the gaps. He'd just stir you up a little bit. And I really don't think he cared whether you became a socialist or whatever. But you certainly would have had exposure to something other than the propagandized versions of socialism.

So Pappenheim was let go and, in my third year, we found ourselves with a black president who had graduated from Talladega, Arthur Gray, a minister and very good speaker, and he and the board of directors had hired as a replacement for Dr. Fritz Pappenheim a black scholar out of the University of Chicago, Lloyd Hogan. And if there was ever poetic justice, it was in that case. Whereas Pappenheim had been a scholar and a theoretician, Hogan was an anarchist who believed that if you did not like what was going on, you should burn the building down. They didn't find out, however. It wasn't in his resume.

Excellent, excellent student of mathematics and was able in addition to money and banking and statistics to continue some of the economic theory. He really called himself an anarchist. I guess I had the feeling after Pappenheim left, there was more of an effort to structure life and activities on the campus along more conservative lines.

This episode around Pappenheim and the changes it generated at Talladega constituted a rather long and bitter struggle in the college. There were several votes taken by the board; there was much correspondence, articles in college publications, too much to describe in detail here. The students' militant action seems to foreshadow campus sit-ins of the later period. This brief summary does, however, give a sense of the climate of the times, and how a small, relatively obscure black college in the deep South was affected by the inquisitorial and intimidating atmosphere of the times.

Ernst Borinski was called a communist and a subversive in the Mississippi legislature and the local press for his activities in the struggle to gain equal rights for African Americans. But more of Borinski later. This and some other instances reveal that the historically black colleges were not immune to this fear, and why should they have been, when the most powerful white institutions, including Harvard, conformed to the pressures and dismissed those scholars who would not "confess" or name names. The only instance I found among the refugees concerns Pappenheim, however.

One response in the report of the Emergency Committee tells us:

Some American scholars are very much aware of over-departmentalization and the lack of integration in this country. To have strengthened the

interest in a more comprehensive approach by continually forcing the issue
in discussions seems to me one of our lasting services the result of which,
however, may only be visible in the long run. . . . [15]

This in answer to the above-mentioned questionnaire by a refugee
scholar. An eastern college reports, in response to the questionnaire:

In spite of the prevalence of the lecture method in European universities,
most of our newcomers were glad to give that method up for the tutorial
and seminar methods. They treated our students as mature people who
came to learn, and they found a genuine response. I mention this fact
because it was an agreeable surprise to me.[16]

One of the significant aspects of the teaching theories and methods
of the refugees as distinguished from their American colleagues was
their ability to teach a broad range of subjects. This was a product of
the European system of liberal education they had pursued, which required languages, and a fair grasp of subjects related to their special
discipline, so that, for instance, an economist could teach sociology. A
number of these scholars had studied law, which enabled them, in some
cases, to teach philosophy, classics, history. Examples are provided by
looking at the roster of the scholars and the subjects they taught:

Ernest Abrahamson, Romance Languages, Latin.
Margaret Altman, animal husbandry, genetics, biology.
Benate Berwin, German, geography, philosophy.
Karl Darmstadter, German language and literature, Russian.
Wolfgang Seiferth, German, Russian.
Gerard Mertens, chemistry, Romance languages.
Joseph Herbert Furth, economics, sociology.
Ernst Manasse, Latin, philosophy, German.
Gustav Ichheiser, social psychology, economics.
Fritz Pappenheim, German, economics.
Frederick Lehner, French, German.

The ability of these financially strapped institutions to have a faculty
member cover several different subjects was, of course, helpful and en-
hanced the refugees' opportunities.

But probably the most significant witness to some of these scholars' teaching comes from interviews with their students. Mr. Jim McWilliams reports in an interview:

> I entered Talladega in 1950 and discovered shortly after I arrived that the faculty was largely white and, to a degree, European. And although I had grown up in Birmingham, Alabama, I had little knowledge of the make-up of the school until I arrived and realized that it was a heavy academic school with little or no sports activity and realized that I was in for a long four years. I was interested in sports, but more interested in academics, so I agreed to the arrangement.
>
> What I also noticed was that the European professors had no problems about extending their classrooms into their homes after classes ended, so that there was no cut-off period between the actual classroom and socializing. And the second thing I noticed was that they did not feel that they could only discuss their particular subject. They were not as compartmentalized as American professors. So that if you had a friendly relationship with a person who taught history, he could just as equally well instruct you in biology or math or talk to you about those things and had no qualms about doing it. So, the total time was an academic atmosphere mixed with classes and social life.
>
> And immediately I had a course with Professor Fritz Pappenheim and we struck it off very well because I scored very high in his classes in economics and could barely survive in German. And he used to tease me about being at the top in one class and barely able to make it in the other. But I think coming from Birmingham, I had never heard anybody speak German or much less any other foreign language, so I had some trouble. Well, I finally managed to survive there.
>
> Professor Pappenheim was a strict disciplinarian in the teaching of German. You had to stand up and answer questions and you didn't know what the questions would be until you stood up and there were exams every Friday. And he walked across the rostrum like a Prussian soldier and would leap over and grab whoever on a given day and students would stand up and try and survive. Incidentally, it was co-educational. As a matter of fact, the girls outnumbered the boys by about six to one because the student body was composed of students who had either been first, second or third in their high schools and, for some reason, the women were beating us throughout the South. I learned to live with the six to one ratio though.
>
> Pappenheim taught economic theory and exposed us very early to classical economics and some of the early scholars in that field. I think that laid the basis for my own further analysis in future years of how important economics is in determining the outcome of people's daily lives and even countries'.
>
> I attended one of those schools in the Birmingham area where the principal comes around in the eighth grade and he says, "do you plan to go to college?" And about 98 percent of us would say no, because we

didn't know anybody who had gone, we didn't have any money. And so, the two people who would usually say yes were the sons and daughters of the minister, the doctor, the funeral director. But the unfortunate thing is that if you answered no, then you got shunted into these very interesting twentieth century courses like cleaning, dying and pressing, and upholstery. And it was there that I was sent. My folks had no money. They were in the steel mills. And so I said no.

By the tenth grade I entered a history class, which was required, and scored the highest in the class. So the teacher there said, "you made a mistake, you should not have answered this thing 'no.'" And so, she was the one who went to Talladega and convinced them that they should let me in there. I had not taken the upholstery. I had taken cleaning, dying and pressing, along with Willie Mays and some other people, who later realized there were some other things to do. Well, she got me into that school on a kind of conditional thing, like, give him a six-month trial. I got the scholarship after the six months, when I started scoring ahead of everybody. After six months, I had scholarships for the rest of my life.

It was a broadening experience on almost every level because you'd enter some of these European homes and they had all kinds of art books, and art on the wall, and different kinds of music and different kinds of food. So, at every direction, I was exposed to different kinds of things and soaking up things that I probably would not have gotten until much later in life. So, I think it was a very fine experience for me and for most of my colleagues there.

You had to develop some kind of rhythm of learning because everybody's taking the same courses and you're going to be faced at the end of the year with exams that cover anything that you could have had. So, there was no way that you could finesse your way out of it. We had essay questions.

Now at your graduation year, they required that you take oral exams and you present some kind of original piece of work that you had done in that four-year period. I don't know anyone in my class who did not become a doctor or a lawyer or an engineer. No exceptions. Many of my classmates who went on to get master's degrees found that to have been an excellent preparation for the thesis.

I was certainly not overwhelmed in the freshman year of law school, like many of my counterparts. And while I later went on into the civil rights movement and concentrated more on that than scholarship, I did select what were considered to be their tough courses at the University of Wisconsin and got the highest scores, so they would never bother me again about whether I came to class.

John Biggers gave a moving account of his conversation with Victor Lowenfeld that provides a sense of the relationship between these two men. I shall now quote from Biggers about Lowenfeld the teacher:

This is a great pleasure for me to speak about Viktor Lowenfeld. Viktor has probably been one of the most important influences in my life as an artist and as an art teacher. The philosophy that he uniquely formulated in art education I feel was a doorway to my own development and to marvelous and wonderful things.

I went to Hampton Institute as a freshman in 1941 from Gastonia, North Carolina, and received a scholarship at Hampton Institute in the plumbing department because I went there to become a plumber. But there had been a stimulation in my family to respect art and music and literature and that type of thing. So, arriving at Hampton to be a plumber, I soon noticed that there was an art class taught in the evening, so I enrolled in this drawing class. Viktor was building an Art Department for the first time. I enrolled in this evening course and truly became so fascinated that I gave plumbing up, which meant a tremendous risk because making a living was extremely important. So, when I enrolled in Viktor's evening drawing class, a new world began.

Living in the South in America at that particular time, the life of my family as well as all the people I knew was greatly restricted because of laws that discriminated against the African American people. So, seeking to extend your own personality and your development, every black child looked for a doorway. So, when Viktor offered this evening class and I enrolled in it, he instructed the class from the point of view of what he called self-expression. Here was an outlet to say something about how one truly felt about life and about the personal frustration, etc.

And his philosophy was that self-expression preceded art expression. So, when one can—can let go and express those very intimate and very close and dear things, whether they are wonderful things or whether they're terrible things, it truly brings one to a sort of normal state so that one can then enter into the meaning of aesthetic expression, you see. So, this was the doorway and this is what happened and it was like magic when this man said, "let expression spring from your environment, how your parents work, what was your family's struggle, how did you make a living, how did you worship," you see. Oh, then this was something that I needed. I needed to say all of this.

So, very rapidly I moved into this and my first picture grew out of the whole atmosphere of that time. War was going on in Europe, but in America there was preparation for it and the people in the South were going to the big cities—the rural people and the small-town people were going to the big cities and going to the North to be employed in defense work. So, migration was the important thing, so my first picture dealt with migration.

My second picture dealt with the gleaners. The gleaners were a family of people who picked up little pieces of coal off the railroad track. Most people burnt coal or wood in their fireplaces and stoves and coal was sold for 25 cents a bucket. But from the train, little pieces of coal would drop along, so these people would gather it along. And having loved

Millet, having loved his *Gleaners*—I had looked at a reproduction during all the time I was in high school. For four years, the *Gleaners* hung in the dining room at Lincoln Academy where I went to high school. So, I had looked at this for four years and had fallen in love with it.

Viktor was entirely different from white Americans. He was completely untypical of any white person I'd ever met. Viktor could hardly speak English. He learned to speak English teaching. Sometimes he would stutter searching for a word for 15 minutes. But in a short period of time he became very fluent. He had been there only one year.

So, Viktor was a man who projected a human quality that was rare for anybody. He has been one of the rare people, and I've met thousands of people—educators, scientists, musicians, artists, ministers—I've met every kind of person. Viktor Lowenfeld still stands out as one of the very great people that I was privileged to meet. He was a true teacher. He projected stimulation and motivation on a level that I have never seen since. He was one of the very rare geniuses that came out of Europe to this country. He was an absolute humanist from the most universal point of view. He knew history. He knew the humanities. He was not only a fine painter himself, but he was a musician, he was a poet.

Viktor was a philosopher, and that's what creative and mental growth is. He had written about the socially handicapped; he said to us one of the reasons why he chose Hampton to come and work in was because the African American people are socially handicapped and he felt a kinship because of his own struggles in Germany (Austria) and what he had just endured there. So, when Hampton Institute came up, he chose it above other schools because of his interests. And he felt that because of the condition of the world, he wanted not only to be a teacher, but he wanted to do something about that. So, to teach people who were, you might say, in a parallel situation that his family and his people were in in Germany, I think he felt that in his way, he would make a contribution.

Whenever he invited me to eat, this was a very human thing. It was like my family relations back home. He introduced me to the European masters of music. We played Bach and Beethoven and Schubert. We played all of this and this is a part of a broadening experience for me. Because when I went there, I knew nothing about classical music. He also learned about American music, gospel, jazz. It was a mutual learning, I hope. He wrote an article there—I believe it was in 1943—it was called "Negro Art Expression in America." In his discussion of Negro art expression, he spoke about the coincidence of modern Western art being motivated and growing out of a consciousness of the aesthetic meaning of African art.

So right off the bat, as a freshman, just as Beethoven was very strange, African art was very strange to me, because I had never seen anything but calendars and cheap reproductions on funeral fans. In our culture, when black represents something that's terrible and bad and the devil, and he picked up these beautiful, these very—I wanted say almost glistening black things—and started telling us the profound meaning of it, the great meaning of African art, its humanistic tradition and how old all this must have been, here was a new experience entirely for me. And right off the bat, I realized that I had a heritage, and inheritance that I was entirely unaware of before coming there. So, suddenly things started truly expanding.

But I do know Viktor came under criticism. Not merely because of the interracial workshops, but the nature of teaching art, the way he taught art. They felt that we should be doing pretty flowers and landscapes and not dealing with self-expression. You had a group of people who had been at Hampton, white people who had been there since the founding of Hampton, who were younger generations of many of the people. They lived isolated lives. They didn't live on campus, they lived in the city of Hampton in a white neighborhood. And these people felt that this would bring change. Hampton Institute has been changed ever since because the self-awareness developed. A rich, very rich change came among the students. They were affected.

He remained a close advisor to me as long as he lived and we had a wonderful relationship. We are talking about the meaning of painting and I spend my time now painting every day and I have several ex-students who are teachers now who paint, too, and we compare our work and discuss the meaning of painting. Lowenfeld and his tremendous insight always comes into the conversation, because painting, as I was stimulated many years ago by him, dealt with layers of meaning, veils of meaning. And when you talk about ways of thinking, you're talking about Viktor Lowenfeld's "Creative and Mental Growth," you're talking about his philosophy. So, it's impossible to discuss the creative act and not discuss Viktor Lowenfeld because that was the nature of his work.

Lowenfeld had taught the blind, both in Vienna and in this country, working with aesthetic principles, including the visual arts.

Another excerpt from the Committee report quotes as follows from an administrator's reply:

In retrospect, it will probably appear that the greatest defect in our whole helter-skelter effort to find new homes for displaced scholars was the lack of any effort to give them an explicit understanding of what the American system of education is all about. If, for example, the Emergency Committee in Aid of Displaced Foreign Scholars had issued a little pamphlet for their indoctrination, much agony might have been saved.

And:

. . . he was able to introduce the students to a world that otherwise would have remained closed to them.[17]

Frederick Gowa taught German at Fisk from 1948–1967. Among other contributions he made, a letter from his widow of March 1990 says the following:

> . . . he was chairman of the Modern Language Department. He helped to bring the Fisk Student International Center to a higher level by introducing play-reading and brought foreign films to the center which attracted the white community to come because there was nothing of that kind available in Nashville at that time. I believe this already helped for better relationship in the fifties and early sixties. Another event was his teaching via Television through a grant given to the University, a first on any campus.[18]

The refugee anthropologist Simon D. Messing received his university education in the United States, which excludes him from this study. Nevertheless, some observations he contributed are worth noting here:

> After completing my course work for the Ph.D. and field work in Ethiopia, I accepted a teaching position at Paine College in Augusta, Georgia (a Methodist-oriented institution with an all-black student body but an integrated faculty) in 1956. At the time an older refugee professor advised against accepting the position on the grounds that this would stereotype me forever a "black college refugee professor." I rejected the advice as obsolete (which it turned out to be) and because I found it ludicrous to know more about Ethiopians than about Blacks of my own country.

Messing now teaches at Southern Connecticut State University in New Haven.

Ruth Fales had some things to say about educational matters:

> On campus, as I guess on most campuses, are the student organizations, the various fraternities. They were always very visible from our house as they went from the dormitories to other buildings where they had their classes. And it was a sight to behold because they would have to go in goose-step, as two forward and one backward and those special hats and be ridiculed. My children, being small, found it very amusing and started to go past them or behind them and imitate them.
>
> But my husband and I were very much against the hazing, of course, and spoke against it. We were told, "you come from a different country, you don't understand. That's the old boys network to get your jobs and so on." And my husband said, how can black people do something ridiculing others like that and asking them to—you know. And he was

strongly reprimanded by some of the other professors, "we just didn't understand."

He also found a very strange reaction from the students when he said in class that "the cradle of civilization was in Africa." And these Americans, black students, they did not like to hear it at all. The other professors, many of them, were not too happy about my husband's type of exam he gave, which was usually not just multiple choice, but essay type, which it seems to me and seemed to him fit for a philosophy course. The professors were not happy about this; it wasn't the students that objected. And, well, that didn't bother my husband too much. He went right on, but it was different from what people were used to.

Walter had urged me to get my American degree and I started taking courses at the university. I had my teacher's degree from Germany. I was the first woman to take a degree. There were women, for instance, faculty wives who took some courses, but not for degrees. So, I was with the class of 1952. I must say the students were very affable. The alumni were very doubtful about the whole thing. The university decided that the charter of Lincoln did not really allow for women students and, therefore, they found two paragraphs in the charter that spoke of males. And they decided they would have to bring it through the courts. It took one year to go through the courts and then I got my degree. So, I graduated with the class of '53 instead of '52.

George Carter also spoke about Fales as a teacher:

The most moving experience I had with Fales was one day we were in a class—there were eight or nine of us in the class—it was very hot, late spring, the windows were open. And he had his foot up on a chair as he was lecturing in a very relaxed fashion and, at some point, he stopped talking and he just stood there. One slowly recognized that he was looking down toward his foot and for a period of I don't remember how long, but long enough for the students in the class to become concerned about the fact that he had stopped lecturing. We all became concerned. It turned out that a white moth had flown in the window and had lighted on the chair where his foot was and he stood there transfixed by this moth. He had an incredible sensitivity.

He had more impact upon me than any other single person on the faculty at Lincoln. I got some real sense of what a European intellectual was like. I got some real sense of the differences in the way he saw history, current events, from the ways in which *The New York Times* talked about them or the way in which some of our more well-respected analysts' publications talked about them. I guess it was Fales through whom I first understood the relativity of point of view, of approach, how peoples' differing cultural assumptions affect the conclusions that they came to.

That stuck with me. I subsequently spent many years in Europe. So that all this became very much real, very much alive. But it was Fales who first showed me that world.

But the kinds of things that I have spent my life being interested in, the kinds of things which are important, it was Fales who—who started that part of my life. In that sense, his impact has been very, very fundamental. The other thing about Fales: I developed at a very young age, 13, 14, years of age, a great sense and feel for and love of what, in this culture, we call classical music. Fales was the cause of whatever it was that drove my interest in music spreading out to other art forms. Now there have been other experiences and people in my life who've certainly contributed to that, but I think that was certainly a beginning. And that part of my life, my interest in philosophy, in literature, music, painting is an area of my life where I deal with the very fundamentals of who and what I am and why it's important to continue to be.

We spent hours sitting on his porch, sitting in the field in the springtime just talking. I remember we had to have an oral examination as a senior and he asked me to choose a subject and I picked Plato. And we must have talked about that for ten minutes. And for the other three or four hours we talked about everything under the sun.

Professor Paul Logan was chairman of the Department of German and Russian at the time I interviewed him in 1988. Here are some of his observations concerning Dr. Wolfgang S. Seiferth, who taught German and Russian at Howard University from 1937 to 1968:

I and a number of other students were very, very close to Dr. Seiferth and I think he looked upon us as his children. I met him as a freshman. At that time I did not know in which direction I wanted to go and he encouraged me and a number of other students to major in German and supported us during our four-year career here and, as a matter of fact, encouraged us to study abroad. He moved me to visit Germany in 1964 and I stayed with a very good friend of his in Wiesbaden and had a very pleasant time there and they gave me a great deal of support. And when I left Wiesbaden, I went to Bad Reichenhall, where I studied three months. And I came back here and I continued my work here with Dr. Seiferth and eventually went to graduate school, and the rest is history.

Dr. Seiferth was a very emotional man, and whenever (recent German history) came up, and whenever these very unpleasant things were broached, it would move him very dramatically and he would often cry. As a matter of fact, I remember very distinctly his love for Goethe and the eighteenth century, that which is called classicism. And I remember distinctly having taken a course in nineteenth-century German literature, but we didn't get out of the Goethe period. We ended with the year 1832, the year of Goethe's death, and we didn't move on, we stayed right there. As a matter of fact, he called his wife Gretchen. It was not her name.

When we took courses in German culture—and I remember his having taught a course in German culture—we never talked about the Nazi period. It was very painful to him. He talked about the Weimar Republic as a very fruitful period. His Germany was something very, very private and something in the past about which he never, never spoke. And as a matter of fact, he was so private that he did not even inform us of the publication of his book. And when I purchased the book and presented it to him for his signature, for an autograph, he was so embarrassed, he just put the book aside, he never signed it. And it's a marvelous book. What he did, he spent his life going to the various cathedrals from the Middle Ages, looking up the representations of *Ecclesia and Synagogue*, the title of his book, and he came to some very interesting conclusions about those representations. It concerns the overlapping between the history of the church and the synagogue.

He was a friend. He never thought that his black charges were inferior. And what he did, he accepted us as human beings, and he encouraged us, and he gave us a great deal of support, but it was never patronizing. And, in effect, he helped us get a sense of self and also self-respect. Some of the ballads by Schiller and some of the very moral issues which were discussed in class, about humanity and how one treats one's fellow man, all that was brought out in very subtle ways in his classes. And I think we, some of us whom he taught, learned him, studied under him are perhaps better people today.

I remember having come back to his office after my first year of graduate school (at the University of Maryland), and he was sitting at this desk and he said, "what do you want to be, Paul?" And I said, "chairman of the German and Russian department," and of course he laughed and I laughed. And here I am, chairman of the German and Russian department.

Dr. Erna Magnus taught social work at Howard University from 1947 to 1966. She was a family friend, and I knew her well. Unfortunately, when I visited her in a senior facility after I had begun this work, she had suffered a disabling stroke and interviewing her was no longer possible. She died soon thereafter in her eighties. I did interview Ms. Marcella Daniels at Howard University, where she had been a secretary in the School of Social Service and told me her recollections of Erna Magnus:

I remember her as a very imposing, stern person; this was a facade. I found out later that this was just her facade and learned that she was a little pussycat, but she never would let anyone acknowledge this to her. I have some little vignettes about her, things that were part of her upbringing, but it was amusing as it unfolded. Things like, she would run and open the door for the dean. And our dean, at that time, she was a very independent woman, almost as stern as Erna. But she would go after her, "Erna, you don't have to do this. This is America, we don't do that here in this country. I can open the door for myself."

And, by the same token, she expected the same type of respect from those of us who were considered under her, you know. And we had to work on this with her to let her know this is a free country. Even though we were secretaries or whatever, we were not servants, we're not in a servile position. And it was really kind of amusing when you look back on it. Because we all knew, also, that it was part of her upbringing, that this was the way things were for her. That very stern, austere German upper-middle-class upbringing. She'd be leaving her cup or something in the little kitchen that we had, expecting the secretaries to wash the cup. Annabelle Burns Lindsey was the dean at the time, and she had to talk about that too. "We wash our own cups here, Erna. These ladies are not servants."

And then I remember her coming through for the students when they didn't have money to pay their fees at graduation time. If they owed a thesis binding fee or a library fee, that would have prevented them from graduating, she would very surreptitiously let them have the money, but not to let anybody know that she would be this kind of softie, you know. It was that kind of thing that would be really kind of hard for her to express. I got very close to her because I knew this. And it was hard for her to expect the kind of thanks that people were inclined to give for that kind of outpouring.

I also know that she was a very stern taskmaster in the classroom. She expected students to learn and she helped them in any way she could to get what they had to learn. And always through this barrier that we don't get too close personally, but her devotion to the students was unparalleled, I think. She really was so set on getting these students through school with the best they could get.

We were all a little more formal then than we are now. We used to call Miss and Mrs. and today, we call everybody by their first name, except the dean. I know the students in Baltimore were devoted to her, because they were the ones who informed me that she had been put in a nursing home when she got so she couldn't take care of herself.

At that time, the University of Maryland didn't have a school of social work, so most of the black and Jewish students would come to Howard, because the only other school of social work in the area was Catholic University. And, at that time, they didn't accept blacks, period. That was back in the 30s and 40s I think. And, of course, with their religious indoctrination, most of the Jewish students didn't want to go there. So, we had a lot of Jewish and black students from the area, and not only Baltimore.

And it was amazing too how she managed with her eyesight. We were fearful when she moved to Baltimore and coming on the train back and forth every day. We didn't know how she managed. We were really afraid for her. She edited all these theses. She read all her own papers from the class, from the students. And she would have to hold the paper about two or three inches from her face, but she never missed a dot. Once we had a secretary in the office who was quite well educated. She had a master's degree. And Dr. Magnus was writing about some Sioux Indians in this country and she spelled it S-u-e, I believe. And Mrs. Moran was her name, said, "Dr. Magnus, this is spelled S-i-o-u-x." "No, no, no, no." She would not accept that at all. Finally she had to get the dictionary to prove to her that this is the way you spell Sioux Indians. And that was very funny, too. I guess it was sort of an arrogance, too. "How can you challenge me," you know. Rigid, that was it, the rigidity, yes.

Some of the faculty would tell us how traumatized she was when she first came to this country. I think she moved to the South when she first came here. But she really could not abide prejudice and the discrimination down there. And, of course, at that time, Jews, blacks and Catholics were just persona non grata down there. I think she was a little reticent about discussing the conditions under which she had to leave Germany and the scattering of her family. And I just have a warm spot in my heart for her.

As I was thanking Ms. Daniels and taking my leave, she had tears in her eyes, and explained that she was so moved remembering Erna Magnus.

I have quoted the Emergency Committee report liberally, because I am certain that the observations cited apply to the refugee scholars in my category, although the racial factor remains unmentioned, except in the paragraph cited above. There are in this connection two items in the report to be noted. In the Appendix, summaries of grants issued to the various institutions list Howard University as receiving two refugee scholars. In the text which covers geographical distribution, we read:

Nineteen grantees found teaching and research opportunities in the District of Columbia, including 5 each at the Library of Congress and the American University, and 3 at the Catholic University.[19]

A small omission perhaps, but in the circumstances not to be ignored: Howard University is left out. Finally, in its concluding paragraphs, we read:

The Emergency Committee was organized in the spirit of the Declaration of Independence. It served as a protest in defense of the dignity of man regardless of race, creed, or political opinion. It was guided by a determination that in the domain of the spirit intolerance and repression should have no place.[20]

It must be said that the Committee rendered an invaluable service to the refugees and one cannot expect it to have transcended the spirit and standards of its times on the subject of race.

The report was also of value because it is clear that the refugee scholars hesitated making negative comments about the black institutions for fear of appearing racist, thus exacerbating the paucity of material caused by the time elapsed. Two surviving scholars I asked for interviews refused, without citing reasons. I am reasonably certain that they had negative feelings about their tenure at a black college, and did not wish to go on record for that reason.

NOTES

1. Stephen Duggan and Betty Drury, *The Rescue of Science and Learning: The Story of the Emergency Committee in Aid of Displaced Foreign Scholars* (New York: The Macmillan Company, 1948), p. vii.
2. Ibid., pp. 102–103.
3. Ibid., p. 140.
4. Ibid., p. 141.
5. Ibid., p. 111.
6. Ibid., p. 69.
7. Ibid., p. 141.
8. Ibid., p. 35.
9. Ibid.
10. Ibid., p. 147.
11. Ibid., p. 148.
12. Ibid., p. 161.
13. Ibid., p. 29.
14. Ellen W. Schrecker, *No Ivory Tower—McCarthyism and the Universities* (New York: Oxford University Press, 1986), pp. 288–289.
15. Ibid., p. 106.
16. Ibid., p. 148.
17. Ibid., p. 161.
18. Ibid., p. 167.
19. Ibid., p. 71.
20. Ibid., p. 191.

CHAPTER 7

Julius Ernst Lips:
"Research Journey into the Dusk"

I have attempted to make as clear as possible from the material at hand that this historical episode at its best and most significant was a two-way street, a learning and enriching experience for the refugee scholars as well as the African Americans whose lives they touched. Above all, I never mean to infer that the negative side of the story is negligible; it simply has not been articulated as much as the positive for reasons which must be understood in their historical, socio-political context.

These chapters on Julius Lips and Ernst Borinski are intended to illustrate two extremes: Borinski, 36 years at Tougaloo College, Mississippi, where he was a truly influential force as teacher and citizen, whose constructive impact is still felt by many people.

On the other side, Lips was a highly controversial figure already in pre-Nazi Germany (and still at the center of scholarly argument in Germany today), at Howard University, and finally in the German-American anti-fascist community in the United States. Julius Ernst Lips was born an "Aryan" in Saarbrücken in 1895. His history remains ambiguous, with contradictory data concerning his positions and achievements. Let it be said that he was a distinguished anthropologist, with a number of remarkable achievements attributed to him. One of his books, *The Savage Hits Back* (Yale University Press, 1937), combines anthropological and art-historical analysis and description, complete with illustrations, and explores the colonized peoples' view of the colonizer. It was considered a significant contribution to the almost

universally poor understanding of the so-called "savages' " perspective
of the European boss.

Lips was a highly intelligent, handsome, charming figure of a man,
perceived by many people he came in contact with as an impressive
scholar and attractive man. After brief service in the German army in
World War I, a record also variously reported, he pursued his studies
at the University of Leipzig, where he was awarded a doctorate in
philosophy, with minors in anthropology and economics, in 1919. In
1923 he received a doctorate in jurisprudence, also in Leipzig. He then
spent time in Frankfurt; his activity there remains unknown. In 1925
he moved to Cologne, where he was employed as an assistant at the
Rautenstrauch-Joest Museum of Anthropology. In 1926–27 he qualified
for ethnology and anthropology at the University of Cologne. In 1929
he was appointed full professor and director of the Museum. These data
are not identical in all records, the consistent problem in tracing Lips's
career.

In 1930 he was sued for plagiarism and a formal complaint was
lodged against him by an employee for gross personal and professional
exploitation and abuse. One of the plagiarism accusers was the anthropologist Paul Leser, a Jewish Ph.D. candidate in anthropology at the
University of Bonn. The aggrieved employee was Dr. Martin Block, a
Jewish Romanian, who was hired by Lips, away from a "secure" position in Bucharest, evidently with many false promises. Block had to flee
from Germany, of course. The lawsuits were settled after the Nazi
takeover with comments to the effect that no law had been broken, but
that the scholar's scientific probity left something to be desired. Lips
had already left for France.

The acrimonious atmosphere around Lips thus had been launched in
1930. Upon the Nazi takeover in January 1933, Lips left the Museum.
According to one faction, because he was a Social Democrat, which
was true; according to another, namely his wife Eva, who described the
occurrences in her book, *Savage Symphony* (New York, 1938), in England, *What Hitler Did to Us* (London, 1938), for his principled stand
against the Nazi dictatorship, as scientist and citizen. Eva Lips's description of her husband makes him such a paragon of perfection in every
respect, that even without the proven inaccuracies in this and other
writings of hers, one harbors doubts about the veracity of her accounts.
Another version tells us of two letters from Lips to the Cologne city

administration, pleading to reinstate him, claiming that all accusations against him were "machinations of a Jewish clique." These letters were quoted in the Nazi press, not a worthy source, after the Eva Lips book caught the Nazis' attention in 1938. There are, however, other, credible sources for these charges, notably a letter dated 1947 from the postwar mayor of Cologne and subsequent curator of the University, Robert Goerlinger, in which he cites the Lips letters to the city authorities and added,

> Yesterday I gained a look at the letters from Julius Lips of 4/19, 7/6 and 7/19/1933, in which he threw himself in the most unworthy fashion at the feet of National Socialism, simply in order to regain his directorship at the Museum and his teaching activity. It was only when this did not succeed, that he went abroad and became a militant opponent of National Socialism.

Goerlinger, who had been a victim of Nazi brutality in a concentration camp, had objected "most strenuously" to Lips's return to Cologne and wrote the letter to Professor Bruno Kuske at the University in order to prevent Lips's return to Cologne in 1947, which he had evidently attempted to do. Professor Kuske had been a Dean of the University during the Nazi period. The letters have not been found so far; they are still being sought by investigators in Germany.

Sources for all this information are: Hans Fischer, "Voelkerkunde im Nationalsozialismus," (Dietrich Reimer Verlag, Berlin—Hamburg, 1990), *Koelner Universitaets Journal*, 20. Jahrgang, Ausgabe 1—1990; and Lothar Puetzstueck, "Von Dichtung und Wahrheit im akademischen Lehrbetrieb, die Entlassung des Voelkerkundlers Julius E. Lips durch die Nationalsozialisten in Koeln 1933," in Wolfgang Blaschke et al., *Nachhilfe Zur Erinnerung—600 Jahre Universitaet Zu Koeln*, (Koeln, 1988).

Lips and his wife fled to Paris, where he did some work, perhaps at the Musée de l'Homme. He wrote to the eminent anthropologist Franz Boas, a secular German Jew, who had come to the United States in 1886. Boas then pursued anthropological studies and became the most significant, influential cultural anthropologist of his time. He taught at Columbia University for the rest of his life. After the Nazi takeover, he became active in the anti-fascist and rescue organizations in New York.

Boas invited Lips to Columbia as a visiting lecturer on a short-term basis. He made some field trips to several Indian groups in the north of Minnesota and Canada and spent time in France in the summers. He apparently had a house on the coast in the South of France.

Our central interest in Lips, however, lies in his two years at Howard University, from 1937–1939. He taught anthropology in the Department of Sociology and Anthropology. He was neither the chairman of the department, nor the founder of the department, nor the founder of an ethnological institute, as he claimed for the rest of his life, in a variety of documents. The department to this day remains the Department of Sociology and Anthropology, and the head of anthropology is the coordinator. Anthropology was already taught at Howard in the early twenties.

Lips's time at Howard was fraught with conflict and acrimony, especially toward the end. An undated memo which we know stemmed from 1937, before he was well known at the University, reads as follows:

Report of Committee on Anthropology:

The Division of Social Sciences of Howard University respectfully requests the Dean of the College of Liberal Arts make the following recommendation to the President and Board of Trustees in its behalf: That Dr. Julius Lips, now Visiting Professor of Anthropology, be appointed Full Professor of Anthropology and Head of a Department of Anthropology, at the expiration of his present appointment.

The Division feels that in the past one of the chief obstacles in broadening and expanding the social sciences at Howard was the absence of Anthropology in the curriculum. Recently, however, this discipline was introduced under the very competent leadership of Professor Julius Lips. The attitude of the Division is that if we are to develop a well rounded program in the social sciences, Anthropology, which is of special importance in the education of Negro students, should be retained and that the creation of a separate department of Anthropology be authorized.

No person of whom we have knowledge is better qualified to undertake this task than Professor Lips. He has demonstrated his understanding of and sympathy with the aims of the various Departments and the problems unique to Howard University. Furthermore, he is a scholar of international reputation. Commenting on Dr. Lips' recent book, THE SAVAGE HITS BACK, Professor Malinowski of the University of London says: "The present book is one of the first contributions to real anthropology, first in rank, first in priority of time." The Division feels that Howard University can ill afford to present courses in this highly technical field except under the competent direction of Professor Lips' calibre and attainments.

                                        Respectfully submitted

                                        Abram L. Harris
                                        E. Franklin Frazier
                                        Emmett E. Dorsey

Two years later, the following letter was sent to the Dean of Liberal Arts:

Dear Dean Thompson:

It is the considered opinion of the Division of the Social Sciences that instruction in Anthropology is a vital and desirable part of the college instruction in the social science field, and thus the Division has repeatedly urged its inauguration and expansion. However, this position is predicated upon the instruction in this subject constituting a program of standard courses of a type and sequence normally offered in American colleges.

In reply to your letter of inquiry concerning the reappointment of Dr. Lips addressed to us as heads of the several social sciences departments concerned, we feel, with regret but upon the basis of concrete experience in the past, that Dr. Lips is unable by his background of experience and perhaps by temperament to participate effectively in the development of such a program.

                                        Sincerely yours,

          (Signed)   Abram L. Harris
                       Department of Economics

          (Signed)   Charles H. Wesley
                       Department of History

          (Signed)   Alain Locke
                       Department of Philosophy

          (Signed)   Ralph J. Bunche
                       Department of Political Science

          (Signed)   E. Franklin Frazier
                       Department of Sociology

Lips was dismissed and, upon the request of a member of the Board of Trustees, given the opportunity to resign. He persisted in claiming that he had resigned before the dismissal, citing the first, 1937 memo

as proof of his standing, without mentioning the time discrepancy or
the later, decisive memo. The white and the black press publicized the
scandal, and Lips was quoted in the *Washington News* and the *Washington Star*, white papers, as well the *Atlanta World*, a black paper,
some of which quotes follow:

The *Atlanta World*, 15 June 1939:
   "I dislike the ethical and scientific approach of the staff members. To
keep out of intrigue and factionalism takes all one's energy and since my
job was to do scientific work, my only recourse was to resign." "Faculty
meetings have a kindergartenish tenor . . . trying to curry favor with Dr.
Johnson (President) one moment and betraying themselves as his sliest
enemies the next." "There is little spirit of helpfulness. And that is a
shame, for the student body on the whole deserves something better. My
association with the students themselves has been a happy one, and for
their sake I can only hope that there will be a housecleaning soon. There
is no friendliness. The professors remain cold and aloof and seem to look
down on the students as though to say, 'you are only a student and I am
a professor, with a Ph.D. degree'."

The article also quotes Dean Charles H. Thompson:

"First, Dr. Lips possesses an unfortunate temperament and personality
which make it extremely difficult, if not impossible, for him to get along
amicably with his colleagues. At the present time, his relationship with
his colleagues in the social sciences is either one of polite indifference or
suppressed hostility, so that any sort of real collaboration is highly im-
probable. Dr. Lips, for some reason has attracted very few students to his
courses, even after a two-year stay at the university. It will be observed
that Dr. Lips has never had more than 38 students during any one of the
five semesters he has been in the college, and during the current year he
had only 15 students the first semester and 16 students are registered
during the second semester."

The other, white Washington papers printed similar stories.

One does not have to be a witness to the world of that time to
understand that a relatively newly arrived European who makes these
comments publicly was not endowed with sensitivity to prevailing racial
politics. Clearly, the information which necessarily reached his New
York backers about this affair must have touched them in a negative
way, given the racial sensibility of a man like Franz Boas. We know

that there was conflict, jealousy and bureaucratic nonsense at Howard, hardly unique to that academic institution, but that does not excuse Lips's mendacity and publicized scorn.

Lips returned to New York without a job. Eva Lips had published her book, *Savage Symphony*, and was able to earn some money by going on lecture tours to speak about their experience in Germany and other topical subjects. Her book had received good reviews. Lips obtained the occasional grant to do field work among the Naskapi and Ojibwe peoples of the North, in Minnesota and Canada.

In 1939 another controversy came to light in the correspondence of the German-American Cultural Association and the Boas correspondence. Lips, a board member of the anti-fascist organization mandated to stand for German culture not tainted by the Nazi brush, made a speech on a German Day Meeting. He attacked the Hitler-Stalin non-aggression pact. Evidently he stopped at a bar after the meeting and was verbally accosted by some unknown men about his political stance, a sensitive subject then, and, in some ways, to this day. He proceeded to resign from the organization, branding it communist and Stalinist dominated. Boas became unwittingly involved in this argument as a fellow board member and had to take a stand. He did not resign. After the Howard debacle, and now the bruising conflict in the exile community, people instrumental in aiding refugee scholars became increasingly skittish about Lips. From 1941 to 1944 there is hardly any information on Lips's activities. The last exchange of letters between him and Boas took place in January 1941. Lips pleaded rather pathetically that he could not survive financially, that he was no businessman, and that his scientific work was not being recognized. Boas replied politely but formally, stating that he would talk to Paul Tillich, at Union Theological Seminary, "to see if there was some way out," but that he personally no longer had access to appropriate funding. Boas died in December 1942 at age 83.

Lips lectured at The New School for Social Research in New York, a haven for many exile scholars, from 1944 to 1948. At some point, after the War's end, an undated, German letter was sent to an unknown official of The New School by Professor Paul Leser, upon his discharge from the U.S. Army. He had been offered a lectureship at The New School and wrote that he would not be able to defend his scholarly honor while teaching in the same faculty with the plagiarist Lips. But as the "case Lips" was well enough known that The New School should have checked the references, it was not his problem. He, Leser, would not interfere with Lips's appointment, considering his serious financial need and the opportunity to make a few hundred dollars. He therefore preferred withdrawing from the lectureship. Paul Leser, of course, was the Ph.D. candidate in Bonn who was party to the plagiarism suit brought against Lips in Cologne in 1930.

All these conflicts and controversies evidently led to increasing awareness of Lips's problematic character and finally made it apparently impossible for him to achieve professional academic status in the United States. The War's end brought the possibility of returning to Germany. Cologne had been excluded, perhaps by the above quoted disclosure; other positions sought in the Allied Occupied Zones appear not to have materialized either.

In 1948 Lips returned to his Alma Mater, Leipzig, also Eva Lips's hometown, in what was the Soviet Occupied Zone, and from 1949, the German Democratic Republic. In 1949 Lips was elected Rector of the University, named for Karl Marx in 1953. This, his last and highest position, surely required some acceptance of Marxist-Leninist, if not Stalinist, ideology, an ironic footnote to his protest ten years earlier against such domination in the New York exile anti-fascist German-American organization. Perhaps the course of history had converted him. He died in January 1950, at age 54. Eva Lips qualified at the University in ethnography and assumed the position of professor in the Julius-Lips Institut Fuer Ethnologie Und Vergleichende Rechtssoziologie established in Lips's name after his death "in consideration of the extraordinary merit of the late Rector of the University of Leipzig." Eva Lips retired in 1966, an Emeritus. She died in 1988 at age 82.

In 1950, Lips's book on the Howard period was published by the Gustav Kippenheimer Verlag in Weimar. Its title, *Research Journey into the Dusk*, was surely never meant for American eyes and was not translated into English. It is "fictionalized" in the most transparent way, calling Howard "Hilltop," the actual name of the campus newspaper. Lips calls himself Smith, Eva becomes Pat Smith, unlikely names for Germans. He invents several grotesque names for colleagues, some of whose models can be recognized even today. He portrays his Howard experience as a fascinating and moving sort of ethnographic field trip, to explore the world of the African American bourgeoisie. Throughout his frequently sardonic descriptions and his astonishing, unscientific conflation of biological and cultural traits, he is the superior European, cultured and refined, generously giving, while observing these unhappy folk:

> Our (his and Eva's) thoughts were in a tangle. In the evening, as we sat together it almost seemed to us as if we had ourselves forgotten what sort of position we were in. And we became increasingly aware that we had embarked upon a strange research journey. This time we were not in Africa, not in Labrador and not in America. But also not with the Negroes, not with the Indians or the Whites. It was a research journey into the dusk.

Dusk, of course, is meant to convey Lips's idea that these unhappy bourgeois, torn from their humble origins, only a generation or two away from slavery, were totally removed and alienated from the poor Negro masses, but not in the white world either. He makes much of the racial characteristics of color and facial feature in these discussions. There is always a good bit of truth in these observations, but these truths are spoiled by their superficial and confused perspective. In a discussion with an African American colleague, Lips describes the following:

> We were agreed that the problem of Negro education was not a problem of "race," but one of social organization, that the bourgeois social structure of America simply is not and will not be in a position to bring a solution to the Negro problem.

Lips's indignant description of the rampant and outrageous segregation practices in Washington were on the mark, as were his observations of the color-prejudicial practices among the Greek letter societies, so dominant in the campus life—fair skin or dark skin color determined many a woman's opportunities, a situation Lips decried. But all of his insights are nullified by his arrogance and his know-it-all certainties, devoid of efforts to explore the very complex depths of the African American experience, difficult, if not impossible for any outsider, let alone for a newly arrived European. The research journey became his reason for having been at Howard; his dismissal is not mentioned.

Lips is an example of a refugee scholar of whom it is difficult to say that his African American encounter had made a constructive impact upon him.

NOTES

1. For information about Lips's years at Howard University, I consulted records at both Howard University and the Moorland Spingarn Research Center in Washington, D.C. Also helpful were the books by Eva and Julius Lips cited in the text.

   The correspondence between Franz Boas and Lips from 1933 to 1942 is in the Smithsonian Institution Anthropological Library, Washington, D.C.
2. Lothar Puetzstueck, a graduate student in Cologne, and I provided one another with much material on Lips. Puetzstueck is preparing his Ph.D. thesis on refugee anthropologists.

   The Karl Marx University in Leipzig also provided information on Lips's brief tenure there from 1948–1950.

Also consulted in the preparation of this chapter:

Lothar Puetzstueck, "Von Dichtung und Wahrheit im Akademischen Lehrbetrieb" in *Nachhilfe zur Erinnerung 600 Jahre Universitaet zu Koeln*, Wolfgang Blaschke, et al., editors (Koeln, 1988).

Westdeutscher Beobachter, 18 & 19 May 1938. (Nazi newspaper)

Posthumously translated and published by Eva Lips: Julius Lips, *Vom Ursprung der Dinge* (Leipzig: VVV Volk und Buch Verlag, 1951), pp. 7–15.

Julius Lips, *Forschungsreise In Die Daemmerung* (Weimar: Gustav Kiepenhaeuer Verlag GMBH, 1950).

Eva Lips, *Rebirth in Liberty 1950* (New York: Flamingo Publishing Co., 1942).

Eva Lips, *Savage Symphony* (New York: Random House, 1938).

Koelner Universitaet, Journal One, 1990 (Koeln), pp. 22–27.

CHAPTER 8

Ernst Borinski: "Positive Marginality" "I Decided to Engage in Stigma Management."

Ernst Borinski was born on November 26, 1901, in Kattowitz, the upper corner of Silesia, Germany, a "three empire corner." His parents were merchants with German loyalties, without very strong feelings about it. His family was Jewish, but not orthodox and Borinski was a secular Jew. This part of Silesia was almost in the war zone during World War I. The town became Polish, and the language in the high school changed back and forth from German to Polish. Borinski found this amusing. In this environment, he learned to speak German, Yiddish, Polish, and Russian. He later added English, French, and Italian. He wanted to study in a German university and did so in Halle, Berlin, and Munich. His maternal grandfather was the first Jewish professor of law in Germany; Borinski made the law his primary study, while also pursuing the humanities and the arts in Munich.[1]

After qualifying in the law, he clerked at the Prussian High Court and subsequently became a magistrate in Kelbra, a small town in Lower Saxony. It was a poor town at a poor time after the war, and one of its main industries, perhaps the only one, was a factory producing mother-of-pearl buttons. Like Tougaloo, it was a world the opposite from the one he had known, as he put it. A case came before him concerning thirty-seven poor people who had stolen all the chickens from a feudal estate belonging to the former Empress. Borinski charged the defendants with a misdemeanor, using the formula of *Mundraub*, translated as "theft of victuals." He chose to convince the prosecutor not to appeal by taking him out for beer and flattery, and succeeded

in persuading him to forget the matter. He later went to the University
of Jena, and worked with the Zeiss Optical Company on issues of labor
law. He was a Social Democrat, represented labor unions and was always active in adult education. Throughout, his goal was to teach in
the best German universities, and all his efforts were focused on that
ambition.

All of this activity and that hope was ended in 1933, of course. Lots
of people knew him, some probably protected him; he enjoyed a leg-
endary reputation and always did many things for many people. He
read and took seriously Hitler's *Mein Kampf* and had discussions and
arguments with Jewish relatives and friends, maintaining that first there
came the Jews' excommunication and then there would follow their
extermination. It was logical, he'd say, "I know history very well."

He obtained a passport and a six-month's visitor's visa to the United
States in 1936, claiming to have no intention to leave Germany. The
Nazis took his passport, and he somehow talked them into returning it
to him. Upon the *Anschluss*, the Nazis' march into Austria in March
1938, he left Germany. He always kept a few thousand Marks, and
simply decided to leave. He took a night express train to Holland, where
controls were very tight. He made a deal with the conductor: For 3,000
Marks and his passport, the conductor agreed to check him out at the
border, without waking Borinski up. It was taking a fearful chance, but
it worked, and he found his passport in the luggage net upon reaching
Holland.

After a stay in England and a wait in Cuba for his immigration quota
number to come up, he arrived in the United States in 1939 and went
to Rochester, New York. There, exploiting his Zeiss experience, he went
to work in the Bausch and Lomb factory, did worker education, and
joined a union. He didn't miss academic work. He became floor manager in a clothing factory and lived with a working-class Jewish family:
"You can make a contribution in any environment." He was drafted
into the U.S. Army, went to North Africa and later functioned as a
translator at Fort Dix, New Jersey.

Upon his discharge, with the help of the G.I. Bill, he studied sociology at the University of Chicago, where he obtained an M.A., then
went for his doctoral studies to the University of Pittsburgh. In 1947,
he accepted a position at Tougaloo College, outside Jackson, Mississippi. He had said that he wanted to go either to Alaska or to Mississippi, and the Mississippi offer came along. He received his doctorate

in 1953, with a dissertation, "The Sociology of Judge-Made Law in Civil Rights Cases."

Upon being asked about his family in Germany, he replied, "I will not speak of family. I have liquidated this area for my mental health."

The above material originates in an audiotaped interview conducted in late 1979 in Borinski's home in Tougaloo by a Jackson lawyer, John Jones, and is deposited in the Mississippi Department of Archives and History in the State Capitol in Jackson. I have conducted interviews with nine people associated in different ways with Borinski. There is a great deal of material on this man; in his thirty-six years at Tougaloo he was involved with countless people as teacher and friend, and his impact was extensive and frequently profound. He was central to the civil rights struggle in Mississippi in a variety of ways, and I shall summarize the most outstanding features I found in the observations of this very varied group.

I want to introduce here these witnesses to perhaps the most important historical developments in the second half of the twentieth century in the American struggle for equality in the deep South.

Professor Richard P. McGinnis, professor of chemistry, came to Tougaloo from Harvard in 1969 and is still teaching there:

When you're a white American, no matter how much you want to say, gee, I didn't grow up in the South, whether you want to or not, you have this sensitivity and you have to bear some sense of history. (And speaking of Borinski) I can't think of anybody that had, in a way that I can't put my finger on, a really profound influence on my life in so many different ways.[2]

Professor George L. Maddox, chairman, University Council on Aging and Human Development, Duke University. Participated at Millsaps College in interracial meetings as faculty in the 1950s, became friends with Borinski in the process of organizing and remained close to him until the end:

Borinski to Maddox: "Maddox, you must tell your students, so they're not misled or disturbed by thinking of black students here as friends. They cannot be because they fully expect to be betrayed." At Borinski's funeral, he spoke and said, "this man transformed my life."[3]

Dr. George Owens, retired; at Borinski's time, first business manager and then president of Tougaloo:

> Ernst Borinski's most important contribution to the life at Tougaloo was his ability to bring outside forces together when—in 1955, Tougaloo was an alien and unwanted college in segregated Mississippi. I was business manager at the time. The Field Foundation made grants to Borinski, and he had the longest strings of renewals on a grant that I've ever known about in history.[4]

Joseph Herzenberg, town council member, Chapel Hill, North Carolina: From 1964 to 1969, at age twenty-three, assistant professor of history at Tougaloo, after obtaining an M.A. from Yale:

> Borinski considered Tougaloo a black Brandeis. While Jews could go to any college now, there was still a role for a Jewish college. Blacks will need black colleges, even after integration. Borinski patronized segregated restaurants in Jackson. I remember his sitting and eating in the Deli restaurant, while a black friend and colleague waited outside in the car. Young civil rights activists, faculty and students, did not patronize segregated establishments.[5]

Professor Jerry Ward, chairman, Department of English, Tougaloo College. Very close friend of Borinski to the end.

> He was displaced from Europe, from a kind of natural, if you want it in quotation marks, ethnic grouping. And I think Ernst maximized this kind of displacement by creating an atmosphere in which white moderates and blacks might debate the issues of segregation, integration, inequality, the movement, world affairs and what have you. He maximized his outsideness as a Jew in Mississippi among blacks without ever overtly appealing, as he might have, to some special notion of kinship. Yet he would be one of the first to say, as he did, I think in 1963, that the Negro student has a right to fail. He never pitied us because we were black and he certainly would not permit us to pity our condition in Mississippi. I'm eternally grateful to him for that.[6]

Frances Coker, professor of sociology at Millsaps College in Jackson, Mississippi. Met Borinski in 1960 while adult student in history at Millsaps, while raising two children. Became close friend.

In my own life, he was one of the most important figures that I can imagine because when I got ready to go back to graduate school, I was going back in history, which had been my undergraduate major, and I was going to the University of North Carolina. And he interceded and told me that I needed to go to Chicago, to the Illinois Institute of Technology, which is where I went. So, he is why I'm in sociology. I didn't even know what it was.[7]

Professor Joyce Ladner, vice-president for Academic Affairs, Howard University, Washington, D.C. Met Borinski in 1961, as a student in sociology at Tougaloo.

He said he had taken the train to Mississippi. He had no idea as to where he was going. He went and looked at the map and saw where it was on the map. He was a man without a past. It was as though he was set down in the middle of Mississippi and he related to it, but he didn't. I will always remember that I didn't have the money for the application fees to graduate schools and they all said, "Dr. Borinski, oh, he paid my application fees to medical school," or to law school. He did that routinely. He used to get grants and he always had a little money available to help students. And he would go into his pocket, as well, and he didn't make very much. I'll tell you, the first person I called when I got my doctorate was Dr. Borinski. Not my mom, not my dad, not my sisters or brothers, but Dr. Borinski.[8]

Reverend Edward King, principal, Edward Brown Elementary School, Jackson, Mississippi. Met Borinski 1954, while undergraduate student at Millsaps College. Became chaplain at Tougaloo and was one of the most militant white civil rights activists in the state. Almost got killed in one of the notorious car chases:

One of the things Borinski had to offer was his differentness and he played on it. He was able to reach many, many people along the way and he could use his foreignness, his otherness to sort of blunder through things where the racial etiquette would say blacks and whites never broke bread together. He was a gentleman of manners and it was very important, so that even when he had reason to be hurt by something other people had done, or angry or upset, there was enormous gentility in how any of that was approached, which was a way of easing and helping with it. It didn't solve anything, but it let you come a little closer to solutions.[9]

Professor Paul Luebke, Department of Sociology, University of North Carolina, Greensboro.

> We were at Tougaloo from 1971 to 1975, my wife Frances M. Lynn and I. She's a political scientist, I a sociologist, and they needed both. We had Woodrow Wilson Fellowships, and Borinski hired us both. It was a time of change, of transition. Borinski was the most important personality at Tougaloo College, certainly in the Social Science Division. He wanted critical thinkers, with a point of view not the ordinary one, which would provoke students into thinking, questioning assumptions. He didn't particularly care about specific points of view, as long as it was in a general humanistic sense, and he could transmit that. By the seventies, there was much more ambivalence on the students' part as to whether or not they had white speakers, whether the white students came from Millsaps College or not. It was the time that the black nationalist idea was still strong on the campus. I mean, by the seventies, a lot of the students at Tougaloo, the blacks at Tougaloo, could care less whether there were any whites on campus or not. My analysis is that he had a hard time with women (in terms of feminist issues). Given the upbringing, given the age, it was one of those egalitarian issues that he had the hardest time with. Yeah, I think he had the hardest time dealing with women as serious intellectual partners.[10]

When Borinski arrived at Tougaloo, he was shown around by Dr. Owens, and when he asked about space for his work, Dr. Owens took him to the basement of a building. It was empty of furnishings, had holes in the floor and was in poor condition all around. Borinski took it and informed some of his social science students of the need for furniture. It is told that the students, ex-G.I.s, used their experience of liberating needed equipment and supplied the space overnight with tables, chairs, desks and other necessary items.

There is a "Personal Vitae of Dr. Ernst Borinski," undated, from which I quote:

> We established a Social Science Laboratory and made Tougaloo, especially the Social Science Division, the center of the activities of the encounters which were called for to change the "Jim Crow" pattern progressively into a modern society based on principles of the American Constitution. I was fortunate to find at Tougaloo a center in which a process of change in the larger community could be initiated and in which progressively the black and the white communities worked on establishing a sound basis for our activities, and I was fortunate enough to help the Tougaloo aca-

demic community, the Jackson community, and the Mississippi communities at large in the renewal of our society thanks to the cooperation and
resources which were made available by the progressive sectors of our
community and by the participation of the regional and national forces
which worked toward ending the segregated patterns in the South. In the
total situation I played my role together with other colleagues and friends
and look at my teaching career at Tougaloo College as a 30-year activity
which could translate my professional insights, my learning, and my
teaching into new social realities for the total community.

Borinski named the area The Lab, generally called "Ze Lab," and it
became the central place for people to gather, all day and into the night.
Borinski had equipped it with books, charts, maps, posters and rows
of long tables and chairs, and, last, but not least, a separate small office
for himself, complete with simple kitchen facilities where food and
drink, usually apple cider instead of the ubiquitous Coke, was prepared
on those special, regular, famous Social Science Forums. These were
generously funded by the Field Foundation and were the only occasions
in Mississippi where black and white could gather together to hear talks
by famous people, among whom were Ralph Bunche, James Baldwin,
Otto Nathan, David Riesman, Pete Seeger, Joan Baez and many others
of interest to a variety of people in the state.

If whites wanted to participate, and many did, they had to come to
the black college, and they did. A typical Borinski device to ensure
mingling of the races was his organizing his students to come a bit early
and occupy every other chair around the table. Thus, white guests had
to sit among blacks, at a table, unheard of for many. Topics were as
varied as the speakers; food and drinks were served after the formal
part of the program, and often the conversation continued late into the
night. The men students could stay as late as they wished; women had
to return to their dormitories by ten o'clock. White women had to be
very careful not to be observed by the representatives of the White
Citizens Councils or the FBI to stay late among black men; it could
lead to lynchings or at least serious harassment of participants. It is
known from the Freedom of Information Act files obtained by Ed King
that license numbers of cars were taken down on occasions of black-
white gatherings, which resulted in nasty telephone threats and worse,
including economic sanctions for people vulnerable to such. The state
secret police function was exercised by an organization called the State

Sovereignty Commission whose central concern was the race issue and the "threat" of integration.

Borinski taught German and Russian classes at Millsaps and brought his Tougaloo students there to share the classes. Other interracial meetings were organized by churches, where Borinski had made it his business to get to know and befriend Protestant and Catholic clergy, including the Catholic bishop, who got involved in the struggle. He also maintained friendly relations with business people and other whites in Jackson who became related to his activities in ways he considered useful. Frances Coker said,

> Ernst became a friend and we went every Wednesday night (to the forums or other interracial meetings). We considered ourselves a moderate community because we weren't doing anything radical, we were just meeting with blacks every Wednesday night. (She is speaking of the early sixties). But our attitudes were different from the rest of the community here. So, Ernst became a friend for this group of white Mississippians. Anybody who came to Mississippi during this era, whether they might be reporters from all parts of the world—not just this country, but international people from everywhere—no matter whom they would call in this city, everybody would tell them to go see Ernst Borinski. So, he was the bridge, in a sense, between the blacks and the whites.[11]

Borinski wrote letters to the editors of the local paper and was heavily attacked as a foreigner and a communist; on 5 December 1955, the Jackson *Clarion Ledger*, whose Mississippi Notebook column by Tom Ethridge featured the Stars and Bars at the head, Borinski was chastised for invoking the law and the Constitution on behalf of integration. Ethridge claimed that crimes were committed disproportionately by blacks, and that therefore Borinski should reserve his legal arguments for his black friends, not attack whites for their lawlessness. In 1957 he was also denounced as "that white radical professor at Tougaloo College" by the Mississippi Legislature.

His obituary in the American Sociological Association's newsletter ironically mentioned this citation among the other honors he received from a number of scholarly societies. All of these attacks, of course, emphasized his foreignness, and his strong accent and "funny" name played a role which at the same time contributed to his ability to get away with activities an ordinary American would have found more difficult and more dangerous, as we know from the violent history of the fifties and sixties.

Some felt that this foreign professor had turned Tougaloo into an oasis, within which The Lab played a special role. Tougaloo also served as a refuge for civil rights activists who needed to hide from their pursuers. Of course, some of these goings-on worried the administration; on the other hand, Borinski brought so much funding—and prestige—from the outside world, that there was no significant interference.

The refugee scholar drew a thoughtful comparison between the White Citizens Councils and the Nazis: Both repressed freedom of expression, both exerted pressure to join, especially on the lower middle-class, both exploited the anti-Semitism found everywhere. The Board of Education in Rankin County, Mississippi, spoke of "Conspiracy of Satan and the Jews" (*Clarion Ledger*). Borinski held that in crisis, frustration reaches easy targets, first the working class, then the middle class. In the South, blacks, in the East, Jews. Two great crimes of Jews and blacks: Jews are not Christians; blacks are not white. As we have seen from the chicken-stealing episode, Borinski took the side of the underdog from early on and throughout his career. His practical approach, such as bribe and flattery, remained a way of dealing with antagonists.

Tougaloo having no graduate divisions, one of Borinski's constant endeavors focused on the placing of promising students into first-rate graduate schools, obtaining financial aid in the form of scholarships or other sources of funding. To this end also, he maintained relationships with colleagues in many universities. He taught summer school at Vanderbilt University, The University of North Carolina, Duke University and Hampshire College in Massachusetts; he also traveled in Europe and Asia. A question asked of him by a colleague, "Ernst, where are your former students now?" was answered simply, "Almost everywhere," which was true. The Southern Sociological Society placed him on its Roll of Honor, only the third selected for this distinction, with the following words in the citation:

> What manner of colleague have we so honored? I have not the time to tell you. Forced to choose a single area of accomplishment, perhaps one must say that he has touched undergraduate lives profoundly through his humane concern evidenced in the wisdom with which he displays good sociology.

The American Sociology Association's newsletter's obituary quotes him,

"Unless we help them (students) go on, everything we do has no meaning." And so he helped students connect with diverse graduate programs and job opportunities all across America. Tougaloo sociology majors had a record of winning Danforths, Fords, Woodrow Wilsons, and ASA Minority Fellowships that compares favorably with the most prestigious schools in America.

One cannot tell about Borinski's life in Mississippi without mentioning the parties which became an integral and "famous" part of the life and the legend. They would include large crowds, music, his "strange" foods, and, most remarkable of all, people from all sorts of backgrounds never likely to socialize together in any other circumstances. Wonderful descriptions of these abound, from programs printed for his later birthday parties and stories told by the lucky participants.

From all of the above it becomes clear that the Tougaloo world he created became not only Borinski's home, but also his family. Frances Coker tells us of the family connection in her experience:

He began to spend his holidays with us and he got to know our extended family, who were very conservative, pro-segregation Mississippians, so this was all very interesting to him and he wanted to know them. And he would give a question now and then that maybe slightly would challenge their point of view, but he never, never took advantage of the situation because he obviously would lose his access. But he went along because he wanted to hear, and see, and he found it all very interesting. And of course, they did too. Imagine, I'm bringing this gentleman to these family gatherings and they never quite could understand that. I think they related to him basically as Jewish who had been kicked out of Europe. And as long as they could do that, and deemphasize this Tougaloo professor of blacks, see, they could stand it.

Ernst loved children. First off, let me say before talking about children specifically, Tougaloo was his family. Tougaloo was his first family. But he loved children and he liked the holidays. And he always brought gifts and he had parties for them, and he loved to observe their progress in whatever it was that they were doing. He was very much in it and encouraged them in any and everything they could possibly do.

And, you see, that is how some of the white children got to know that there was a biracial community here. He expected you to be able to bring your children. And he was a moderating influence in families. When you would have trouble with your teenager or something, you know, he would always see the fun part of it or he would laugh. He had very interesting insights if you were having family difficulties. So that he was a manager, not just of things at Tougaloo, but he was a manager of this family that he was a part of. Everywhere he went, he was a manager. Oh, the kids loved him. They would always expect him to be included in any family activities.[12]

There are two other characteristics of this remarkable man which were brought out by several respondents: His ever-ready sense of humor and his amazing optimism in the presence of the most dismal and terrifying situations, especially also remembering the German experience. He considered a sense of optimism about the world as essential to any activism; at least that is the inference that comes to mind.

Joyce Ladner remembers his aloneness thus:

He was alone and a loner, in a very real sense, even though he had lots of people come out to the campus to visit with him. He had people in to dinner often. But for the most part, he was alone. I can visualize him walking across the campus early in the morning from his private quarters in one of the dormitories—he had a suite, I guess—and he would walk across the campus by himself. And late at night, you'd see him again, walking by himself.[13]

He died on May 26, 1983. He didn't interrupt anything. He had finished teaching at Tougaloo, which he never stopped doing, and was getting ready to go to his summer school assignment at Vanderbilt University. And two of "his families" were expecting babies that week. Here is Frances Coker's account:

We were to go over there for supper that Wednesday night, and that morning he went to the hospital, and he said, "you know, I'm really sick. I don't know, they can't find what's wrong." And he died on Friday. And the interesting thing is he died the week after my granddaughter was born and he had invited us all to supper after my daughter came home from the hospital. And he called her at the hospital and sent some flowers when the baby was born and all that. And the other family had had a grandchild born the week or two before that. And it was like he kept waiting for these grandchildren to be born. I kind of think he wasn't going to die till these children were born. He didn't have any health problems really. Well, my daughter had just gone home from the hospital and when she got up, that was the first place she went [Borinski's bedside].[14]

Jerry Ward tells,

When I went to see him at the hospital the week he died, he said, "well, I've had a very long and happy life and all of my systems seem to be giving out, so I think it's time to go."[15]

He is buried in the little cemetery on the campus, and on his grave-stone there is a Star of David.

The ASA obituary is worth quoting here in part again:

A memorial service and celebration of his life will be held at Tougaloo October 21; donations can be sent to the Ernst Borinski Fund, to endow a scholarship fund in his honor. His never-failing optimism was summed up in his aphorism: "What people haven't learned, they do not know." Ernst used that phrase to restrain frustrated Northern liberals who wanted to teach probability theory, from blaming rural black Mississippians for not knowing algebra, and by using it, he located the problem where it belonged—with the anti-intellectual white-dominated public schools, not within the family background of their victims. In his career in Mississippi, Borinski made magnificent use of his own background and status, which he called "positive marginality." In his words, "I came to Mississippi with full awareness of this otherness and felt this otherness strongly as a stigma. I felt stigmatized culturally, attitudinally, behaviorally, racially and linguistically. I decided to engage in stigma management and to deal positively with my otherness."

NOTES

1. Much of the information on Dr. Borinski came from my interviews with his students and colleagues, as well as documents and letters obtained at Tougaloo College.

   An audiotaped interview with Dr. Borinski conducted by John Jones at Borinski's home in 1979 is on file at the Mississippi Department of Archives and History in the state capital in Jackson, Mississippi, in addition to other documents from Tougaloo College.
2. Interview with Richard McGinnis on May 10, 1987, at his home in Edwards, Mississippi.
3. Interview with George Maddox on May 24, 1985, at Duke University, Durham, North Carolina.
4. Interview with George Owens on May 9, 1987, at his home in Jackson, Mississippi.
5. Interview with Joseph Herzenberg on May 23, 1985, at his home in Chapel Hill, North Carolina.

6. Interview with Jerry Ward on May 30, 1985, at the Smithsonian Institution, Washington, D.C.
7. Interview with Frances Coker on May 9, 1987, at her home in Jackson, Mississippi.
8. Interview with Joyce Ladner on June 16, 1988, at her home in Washington, D.C.
9. Interview with Ed King on May 23, 1988, at my home in Washington, D.C.
10. Interview with Paul Luebke on May 24, 1985, at his home in Durham, North Carolina.
11. Op. cit., interview with Frances Coker.
12. Ibid.
13. Op. cit., interview with Joyce Ladner.
14. Op. cit., interview with Frances Coker.
15. Op. cit., interview with Jerry Ward.

LIST OF REFUGEE SCHOLARS

Atlanta University, Atlanta, Georgia
Ossip Flechtheim, 1940–43: History, Political Science
Hilda Weiss, 1941–43: German, Social Studies

Bennet College, Greensboro, North Carolina
Beate Berwin, 1942–50: German, Geography, Philosophy

Central State University, Wilberforce, Ohio
Gertrude Engel, 1951–55: English

Coppin State College, Baltimore, Maryland
Eric Fisher, 1965–69: Geography

Dillard University, New Orleans, Louisiana
George Iggers, 1957–63: History
Wilma Iggers, 1957–63: French, German

Fisk University, Nashville, Tennessee
Gisella Cahnmann, 1943–45: French
Werner Cahnmann, 1943–45: Sociology, Economics
Ferdinand Gowa, 1948–67: German
Elsbeth Einstein Treitel, 1943–46: German
Otto Treitel, 1943–46: Mathematics, Physics

Hampton Institute (now University), Hampton, Virginia
Margaret Altman, 1941–56: Animal Husbandry, Genetics, Biology
Peter Kahn, 1953–57: Art
Karla Longree, 1941–50: Home Economics

Ernst Lothar, 1948–50: Art
Marianne Lothar, 1948–50: German
Viktor Lowenfeld, 1939–46: Art
Hans Mahler, 1941–43: Music
Fritz Neumann, 1946–47, History
Anna Stein, 1942–44: Mathematics

Howard University, Washington, D.C.
  Ernest L. Abrahamson, 1939–41: Romance Languages, Latin
  Kurt Braun, 1943–69: Economics
  Johann Caspari, 1946–53: German
  Karl Darmstadter, 1945–65: German Language and Literature,
    Russian
  John Herz, 1941–43 & 1948–52: Political Science
  Gerhard Ladner, 1951–52: Art History
  Julius Ernst Lips, 1937–39: Anthropology
  Erna Magnus, 1947–66: Social Work
  Otto Nathan, 1946–52: Economics
  Franz Julius Rapp, 1945–51: Art History
  Hugo B. Schiff, 1943–50: Jewish Literature and Cultural History
  Wolfgang Seiferth, 1937–68: German, Russian
  Erika Thimey, 1944–55: Dance

Knoxville College, Knoxville, Tennessee
  Gerard M. Mertens, 1957–62: Chemistry, Romance Languages

Lincoln University, Lincoln, Pennsylvania
  Walter Fales (Feilchenfeld), 1946–53: Philosophy
  Josef Herbert Furth, 1939–44: Economics, Sociology
  Simon Green (Gruenzweig), 1948–51: Mathematics

North Central University, Durham, North Carolina
  Adolf Furth, 1952–62: Chemistry
  Christa Furth, 1952–62: German
  Ernst Manasse, 1939–73: German, Latin, Philosophy
  Marianne Manasse, 1948–49 & 1956–72: German
  Hilda Weiss, 1940–41: Social Studies

Paine College, Augusta, Georgia
  Simon D. Messing, 1956–58: Anthropology, Sociology, History

Philander Smith College, Little Rock, Arkansas
  Simon Green (Gruenzweig), 1952–55: Mathematics
  George Iggers, 1950–56: History
  Wilma Iggers, 1950–56: French, German

Saint Augustine College, Raleigh, North Carolina
  Adolf Furth, 1963–66: Chemistry
  Christa Furth, 1963–66: German

Spelman College, Atlanta, Georgia
  Hilda Weiss, 1941–43: Social Studies

Talladega College, Talladega, Alabama
  Gustav Ichheiser, 1944–48: Social Psychology, Economics
  Herman Kranold, 1936–43: Economics
  Gerhard M. Mertens, 1952–53: Chemistry
  Fritz Pappenheim, 1944–52: German, Economics
  Lore May Rasmussen, 1949–55: Elementary Education

Tougaloo College, Tougaloo, Mississippi
  Ernst Borinski, 1947–83: Sociology, German, Russian

Virginia Union University, Richmond, Virginia
  Marie H. Gunther, 1950–65: German, Geography

West Virginia State College, Institute, West Virginia
  Frederick Lehner, 1939–61: French, German

Xavier University, New Orleans, Louisiana
  Katherine Radke, 1935–38: Director, School of Social Service
  Wolfgang Johann Weilgarth, 1945–49: German
  Erwin Wexberg, M.D., 1936–40: Social Psychiatry

LIST OF INTERVIEWS CITED

JOHN BIGGERS, 17 May 1988, at his home in Houston, Texas.
GEORGE CARTER, 13 June 1985, at his home in Scarboro, New York.
FRANCES COKER, 9 May 1987, at her home in Jackson, Mississippi.
RUTH FALES, 13 February 1990, at Lincoln University, Lincoln, Pennsylvania.
JOHN HERZ, 13 June 1985, at his home in Scarsdale, New York.
JOSEPH HERZENBERG, 23 May 1985, at his home in Chapel Hill, North Carolina.
ED KING, 23 May 1988, at the author's home in Washington, D.C.
JOYCE LADNER, 16 June 1988, at her home in Washington, D.C.
PAUL LOGAN, 4 August 1988, at Howard University in Washington, D.C.
PAUL LUEBKE, 24 May 1985, at his home in Durham, North Carolina.
MARCELLA McDANIELS, 15 June 1988, at Howard University.
RICHARD McGINNIS, 10 May 1987, at his home in Edwards, Mississippi.
JIM McWILLIAMS, 13 May 1984, at the Smithsonian Institution in Washington, D.C.
GEORGE MADDOX, 24 May 1985, at Duke University, Durham, North Carolina.
ERNST M. MANASSE, 2 April 1991, at his home in Durham, North Carolina.
GABRIEL MANASSE, 27 June 1988, at the author's home.
SIMON D. MESSING, 8 November 1984, at the Smithsonian Institution.
GEORGE OWENS, 9 May 1987, at his home in Jackson, Mississippi.
SUSAN RIPLEY, 27 October 1987, at her home in Fairfax, Virginia.

ERIKA THIMEY, 1 November 1988, at her home in Smithsburg, Maryland.
JERRY WARD, 30 May 1985, at the Smithsonian Institution.
GROUP INTERVIEW, 12 February 1990, at Lincoln University.
  Participants: Ruth W. Fales, Dorothy Jones, David Swift, Dorothy and Andrew Murray, Emery Wimbish, Jr., Mary and Alfred Farrell, Isaac S. Mapp.

BIBLIOGRAPHY

Anderson, James D. *The Education of Blacks in the South*, Chapel Hill: University of North Carolina Press, 1988.

Bentwich, Norman De Mathos. *The Rescue and Achievement of Refugee Scholars*, The Hague: Nijhoff, 1953.

Breitman, Richard and Kraut, Alan M. *American Refugee Policy and European Jewry, 1933–1945*, Indianapolis: Indiana University Press, 1987.

Bond, Horace Mann. *Education for Freedom, A History of Lincoln University*, Princeton, 1976.

Boyers, Robert, ed. *The Legacy of the German Refugee Intellectuals*, New York: Schocken Books, 1972.

Bullock, Henry Allen. *A History of Negro Education in the South*, Cambridge: Harvard University Press, 1967.

Coser, Lewis A. *Refugee Scholars in America: Their Impact and Their Experiences*, New Haven: Yale University Press, 1984.

Crawford, Rex W. *The Cultural Migration: The European Scholar in America*, New York: Arno Press—A New York Times Company, 1972.

Davie, Maurice R., et al. *Refugees in America—Report of the Committee for the Study of Recent Immigration from Europe*, New York: Harper, 1947. (Reprint: Greenwood Press, Westport, Conn., 1975.)

Duggan, Stephen and Drury, Betty. *The Rescue of Science and Learning*, New York: The Macmillan Company, 1948.

Fermi, Laura. *Illustrious Immigrants*, Chicago: University of Chicago Press, 1968.

Fleming, Donald and Bailyn, Bernard, eds. *The Intellectual Migration—*

Europe and America 1930–1960, Cambridge: Belknap Press of Harvard University, 1969.

Fosdick, Raymond, B. *The Story of the Rockefeller Foundation*, New York: Harper and Bros., 1952.

Fosdick, Raymond, B. *Chronicle of a Generation*, New York: Harper and Bros., 1958.

Gramm, Hanns. *The Oberlaender Trust 1931–1953*, Philadelphia: Carl Schurz Memorial Foundation, 1956.

Greeley, Andrew M. *Ethnicity in the United States: A Preliminary Reconnaissance*, New York: John Wiley & Sons, 1974.

Ginzberg, Ralph. *One Hundred Years of Lynchings*, New York: Lancer Books, 1969.

Heilbut, Anthony. *Exiled in Paradise*, New York: Viking Press, 1983.

Herz, John. *Vom Ueberleben*, Dusseldorf: Droste, 1984.

Hobson, Julius. Memorial Service Program, 1977.

Jackman, Jarrell and Borden, Carla, eds. *The Muses Flee Hitler*, Washington, D.C.: Smithsonian Press, 1983.

Jahrbuch fuer Amerikastudien, Heidelberg: Band 10, 1965.

Jay, Martin. *Permanent Exiles—Essays on the Intellectual Migration from Germany to America*, New York: Columbia University Press, 1985.

Johnson, Alvin. *Pioneers Progress—An Autobiography*, New York: Viking Press, 1952.

Kampe, Norbert. *Studenten und Judenfrage im Deutschen Kaiserreich*, Goettingen: Vandenhoeck & Ruprecht, 1988.

Kent, Donald Peterson. *Refugee Intellectuals—The Americanization of the Immigrants of 1933–1941*, New York: Columbia University Press, 1953.

Koelner Universitaet, Journal One, Koeln: 1990.

Krohn, Klaus Dieter. *Wissenschaft im Exil*, New York: Campus, 1987.

Kuklick, Bruce. *The Rise of American Philosophy*, New Haven: Yale University Press, 1977.

Lewis, David Levering. "Parallels and Divergences: Assimilationist Strategies of Afro-American and Jewish Elites from 1910 to the Early 1930s," *Journal of American History*, Vol. 71, No. 3, December 1984.

Lips, Eva. *Rebirth in Liberty*, New York: Flamingo Publishing Company, 1942.

―――. *Savage Symphony*, New York: Random House, 1938.

Lips, Julius E. *Forschungsreise in die Daemmerung*, Weimar: Gustav Kiepenheuer Verlag GMBH, 1950.

―――. *Vom Ursprung det Dinge*, Leipzig: VVV Volk und Buch Verlag, 1951.

Moeller, Horst. *Exodus der Kultur*, Muenchen: C. H. Beck, 1984.

Ploetz. *Das Deutsche Kaiserreich*, Freiburg: Verlag Ploetz, 1984.

Protokoll des II. "Internationalen Symposiums zur Erforschung des deutschsprachenigen Exils nach 1933," hrsg. v. Deutschen Institut der Universitaet Stockholm, 1972.

Puetzstueck, Lothar. "Von Dichtung und Wahrheit im Akademischen Lehrbetrieb," in *Nachhilfe zur Erinnerung 600 Jahre Universitaet zu Koeln*, Wolfgang Blaschke, et al., eds. Koeln: 1988.

Radkau, Joachim. *Die deutsche Emigration in den USA: Ihr Einfluss aud die amerikanische Europapolitik, 1933–1945*, Duesseldorf: Bertelsmann Universitaets Verlag, 1971.

Roscoe, Wilma J., ed. *Accreditation of Historically and Predominantly Black Colleges*, Lanham, Md.: National Association for Equal Opportunity in Higher Education, University Press of America, 1989.

Rurup, Reinhard. *Emanzipation und Antisemitismus*, Goettingen: Vandenhoeck & Ruprecht, 1975.

Sayen, Jamie. *Einstein in America*, New York: Crown Publishers, Inc., 1985.

Schrecker, Ellen W. *No Ivory Tower: McCarthyism and the Universities*, New York: Oxford University Press, 1986.

Strauss, Herbert, et al., eds. *International Biographical Dictionary of Central European Emigres, 1933–1945*, New York: 1983.

―――. *Jewish Immigrants of the Nazi Period in the USA*, Vol. 2, Classified and Annotated Bibliography, New York: 1984.

Synott, Marcia Graham. *The Half-Opened Door*, Westport: Greenwood Press, 1979.

Taylor, John R. *Strangers in Paradise*, New York: Holt, Rinehart & Winston, 1983.

The Negro Yearbook, Tuskegee: Tuskegee Institute, 1932.

Wedlock, Lunabelle. *Reaction of Negro Publications and Organizations to German Antisemitism*, Washington, D.C.: Howard University Press, 1941.

Weisbord, Robert S. and Stein, Arthur. *Bittersweet Encounter: The Afro-American and the American Jew*, Westport: Negro Universities Press, 1970.

Westduetscher Beobachter, 18 & 19 May, 1938.

Wetzel, Charles J. *The American Rescue of Refugee Scholars and Scientists from Europe, 1933–1945* (Ph.D. Dissertation), Madison: University of Wisconsin, 1964.

INDEX